E. H. D

PAUL AND HIS TEACHINGS

PAUL
and His Teachings

FRED L. FISHER

BROADMAN PRESS · NASHVILLE, TENNESSEE

© Copyright 1974 · BROADMAN PRESS
All rights reserved
ISBN: 0-8054-1339-1
4213-39

Library of Congress Catalog Card Number: 73-83829
Dewey Decimal Classification: 227
Printed in the United States of America

CONTENTS

Preface   vii

Part I   Paul: Theologian in the Making
     1. The Jew   11
     2. The Convert   29
     3. The Christian   41

Part II   Paul: Adversary of the Judaizers
     4. The Course of the Conflict   66
     5. Dead in Sin   75
     6. Salvation by Grace Through Faith   85
     7. Life in Christ   103
     8. Living in Christ   119

Part III   Paul: Opponent of the Gnosticizers
     9. The Questions   137
     10. Paul's Answer   148

Index to Theological Subjects   160

I dedicate this book
to my two lovely granddaughters:
LISA ANN MAXSON and **DELANNA LYNN FRYAR**
with the prayer that they will come to know, love, and
serve the Christ whom Paul preached.

PREFACE

What could possibly justify another book on Paul? Paul is certainly not a neglected subject. Books and articles on him abound by the hundreds. Nor can I claim to have new insight into Paul's teaching or knowledge concerning his life; but I have tried to give a new organization to the material. If there is anything creative about this book, this must be it. When the teaching of Paul is matched with his own experience, its relevance becomes clearer.

Two things may justify another attempt to speak of Paul. First, his importance in the Christian beginnings cannot be denied. For good or bad, Christian theology and practice has received an indelible imprint from the mind and heart of the apostle. If anyone wants to understand Christianity, he must not neglect Paul. Jesus is central and his teachings basic, but it was Paul who, more than any other one person, publicized, if he did not create, the Christian view of Christ, his work, his church, and his gospel.

Second, a book on Paul, if it leads to greater understanding, is justified by Paul's relevance to modern religious life. Paul is not the only man who ever faced problems in his ministry, but he was the first man who faced many of them. Led by the Holy Spirit, he faced them in a creative way which forms a pattern for us to follow. The Judaizers and the Gnosticizers were not the only heretics to arise in Christian history, but they were the first ones. Most of the heresy of the ages is contained, in principle, in these two heresies. It was no accident that the Protestant Reformation and the Wesleyan revivals were instigated by men who listened to the voice of Paul.

Opinions have been varied about Paul. Some individuals have looked on him as the hero of the Christian faith, one who can lead us more surely than any other to true Christian devotion. Others have looked upon him as one who distorted and destroyed Christian theology, a man to be shunned and rejected. One thing is sure; Paul cannot be ignored. His voice may be muffled at times; it cannot be stilled. In my opinion, this is one of the brightest hopes for the future of Christianity in our world.

The voice of Paul still rings out with God's thunder against all those who would:
> make Christ less than God,
> deny the full humanity of Christ,
> deny the finality and power of the cross,
> think to supplement Christ's revelation of God,
> speak of more than one true God,
> attempt to play off the justice of God against his love,
> shut God up in the world and make him one of us,
> shut God out of the world and make him irrelevant,
> deny the eternal purpose of God,
> make God a stern sadist with no mercy,
> make God a loving God with no justice, or
> try to mix grace and law.

It rises in protest against those who would:
> try to mix faith and works,
> ascribe any merit to man,
> propose spiritual improvement by human achievement,
> say that man is lost because he is a man,
> deny that man is essentially a sinner,
> seek to receive Christ as Savior without receiving him as Lord,
> deny that salvation is a "now thing,"
> deny that salvation is a "yet-to-be thing,"
> exalt knowledge over faith, or
> separate the Holy Spirit from Christ.

His voice continues to challenge those who would:
> make legalism a way of Christian living,
> claim that salvation by grace encourages sin,
> claim that the Christian is free from all restraint,
> deny that "everyday life" has spiritual meaning,
> substitute a system of "human regulations" for responsible Christian freedom,
> promote asceticism as a way to superior goodness,
> find in visions a knowledge contrary to that revealed in Christ,
> substitute emotional spiritualism for responsible living and service,
> deny the dignity and meaning of the local churches,
> think to live an isolated Christian life,
> use the church as a shield against God and men,

PREFACE

live in the church without seeking the good of their fellowmen, and be "superficial" and "ritualistic" in their worship of God.

We need to hear Paul's voice today. May this book contribute to that!

Most scriptural quotations are from the Revised Standard Version in this book. Quotations from foreign language works are usually my own paraphrased translation. Standard notations have been used; *op. cit.* is sometimes replaced by abbreviated titles to avoid confusion. Standard works of reference and theological journals are sometimes referred to by their common abbreviations, as below.

Abbreviations

Acts of God	Wright and Fuller, *The Book of the Acts of God*
Faith	Conner, *The Faith of the New Testament*
Foundations	Fuller, *Foundations of NT Theology*
IDB	*Interpreter's Dictionary of the Bible*
JBL	*Journal of Biblical Literature*
Lectures	Schweizer, *Lectures at the University of Zurich*
NTS	*New Testament Studies*
Outline	Conzelmann, *An Outline of the Theology of the NT*
Perspectives	Käsemann, *Perspectives on Paul*
Predecessors	Hunter, *Paul and His Predecessors*
Problem	Wilson, *The Gnostic Problem*
TDNT	*Theological Dictionary of the New Testament*

PART I
Paul: Theologian in the Making

1
THE JEW

Paul was first of all and always (though not always first of all) a Jew. Neither his life nor his thought can be understood apart from his Jewishness. He saw Christianity as "the true and final form of Judaism" not as a new religion completely different from it.[1] He brought to his Christian life a whole panoply of matured theology, custom, practice, and prejudice—all of it Jewish.

He never ceased to think of himself as belonging to God's people (Rom. 11:1-6). His continual concern was for the conversion of his fellow Jews (Rom. 9:1-5; 10:1-4). He practiced his Judaism throughout his life and expected Jewish Christians to remain loyal to the Law.[2] He preached the gospel in Jewish terms; his vocabulary was sprinkled with terms familiar to every Jew—the law, faith, the promises, the righteousness of God, the judgment, the Spirit.[3] Of course, his Christian interpretation of these themes was quite unacceptable to his fellow Jews. In spite of that, we need not hesitate to call him the great Jew-Christian.[4]

I. The Jewish Heritage

Paul boasted of his Jewish heritage; he felt the Jew had a head start in life, an advantage in his relation with the living God. "Again and again there breathes through the thought of Paul his pride and joy in the privilege of being a Jew, one of the chosen people of God."[5] He insisted that he "had reason for confidence in the flesh" because of his exemplary life in Judaism (Phil. 3:4). Though his desire to know Christ led him to renounce these fleshly advantages, he prized them. He declared that both Jew and Gentile rightly rested under the judgment of God. When asked by his Jewish opponent, "What advantage has the Jew?" Paul replied: "Much in every way. To begin with, the Jews were entrusted with the oracles of God" (Rom. 3:1-2). He did not mean that the Jew was not condemned; he was; the power of sin ruled in his life (Rom. 3:9). He meant that the Jew had an advantage over the Gentile.

This advantage consisted mainly in the special revelation of God through Adam, Abraham, Moses, David, and the prophets. To the Israelites and to them alone "belong the sonship, the glory, the covenants, the giving of the law, the worship, and the promises; to them belong the patriarchs, and . . . from them according to the flesh," Christ had been born (Rom. 9:4–5).

1. Of the Tribe of Benjamin

Paul was wellborn. In religion, he yielded ground to no man. He was a descendant of Abraham which meant that he had absolute racial purity (Rom. 11:1; 2 Cor. 11:22).[6] He was an Israelite, not an Ishmaelite; thus he belonged to "the chosen people, the covenant nation" (Rom. 11:1; Phil. 3:5; 2 Cor. 11:22).[7] The genealogical tables had been preserved in his family; he could know that he was of the tribe of Benjamin (Rom. 11:1; Phil. 3:5).

If we can trust Acts, Paul was born in Tarsus of Cilicia (Acts 22:3; 21:39), had both a Jewish name—Saul—and a Roman name—Paul. This would indicate that his family was wealthy and had high standing in the Roman community.

2. A Hebrew of the Hebrews

From the little information we have about the boyhood of Paul, a few things can be deduced. He was a "Hebrew born of the Hebrews" which meant that his family, though a part of the dispersion, had preserved the customs and spoke the Hebrew language (Phil. 3:5).[8] One such custom was circumcision on the eighth day after birth. We can be sure that Paul received regular training in the Mosaic law and that his family regularly attended the Jewish synagogue in Tarsus. The services there would have been conducted in Greek, using the Greek translation of the Old Testament (the Septuagint). Thus Paul was a bilinguist from his boyhood.

Jewish boys learned a trade, a way to earn a living by the use of the hands. This was true regardless of the economic status of a family. Paul learned his—tentmaking. He used his trade to support himself (and perhaps his co-workers) as a Christian missionary (Acts 18:3; cf. 1 Thess. 2:9; 1 Cor. 4:12; 2 Cor. 11:27).

What did Paul look like? What were his physical characteristics? Of such things, we know little. A second-century source describes him as small in stature, bald-headed (but of course not as a boy), bowlegged, of vigorous physique, with meeting eyebrows and a slightly hooked nose.[9]

No beauty pageant Adonis he! The hardiness of his physique is attested by the severe trials and labors which he encountered in his ministry. Because he frequently used illustrations from the arena, Paul seemed interested in athletic events and may even have participated in them.

What of his spiritual growth? Nothing is known for sure except that it led to an exemplary life in Judaism. Perhaps a hint is contained in the words: "I was once alive apart from the law, but when the commandment came, sin revived and I died" (Rom. 7:9). Does this point to a traumatic experience in the life of Paul, the boy? I think it does. Caution is indicated because there is no consensus on this point among scholars, but the words seem to carry the poignancy of personal remembrance. If so, they point to a depth of conviction of sinfulness which ruled Paul's life both as a Jew and to a lesser extent as a Christian. They speak of the pride of a Jewish boy who learned the law by heart and prided himself in it, thinking that through it he had life. Then something happened. Perhaps a neighbor boy got a pony for his birthday and Paul coveted it. When he did, sin rose up and pointed an accusing finger at him, reminding him of the commandment, "Thou shalt not covet." Paul realized that he was a sinner. No longer did the law have the savor of life unto life, but of death unto death. His great zeal for the law, of which he often spoke, could have arisen from his determination to atone for his sin and win the approval of God.

3. A Pharisee

Was Paul a Jewish rabbi? The evidence is mixed, but an affirmative answer seems indicated. The book of Acts tells us that he was trained at the feet of Gamaliel, the great Jewish liberal of that day (Acts 22:3). Some deny the truth of this statement, pointing to Paul's fundamentalism as a Jew and thinking it unlikely that he learned his rabbinics from such a liberal teacher.[10] On the other hand, his way of using the Old Testament and the form of some of his arguments show a high level of training in rabbinics which harmonize with this tradition. Further, Paul's thought as a Christian is rooted in the rabbinic world of thought and shows him to be "a rabbi become Christian."[11] If the tradition is true, Paul, probably at the age of fourteen, came to Jerusalem and spent several years in such study.

Was Paul a married man? If he was a Jewish rabbi, he probably was and had a family of his own. Marriage was considered a religious duty and Paul could hardly have been "blameless" (Phil. 3:6) if he were not married. If he were married, what happened to his family? Either his wife died or left him when he became a Christian. Certainly he did not have a wife when he wrote Corinthians. He was living a celibate life. We cannot be dogmatic about this. Those who think that Paul was a crabby old bachelor who thought little of marriage and knew even less of it will be able to argue for their conclusions. Those who think that he had had a tragic married experience, spoke highly of marriage, and was extremely sensitive to its problems can with equal reason (better, I think) argue for their conclusions.

Was Paul a Pharisee? He tells us that he was (Phil. 3:5). This meant that he was a member of that fraternity of Jews who were uncompromising legalists. His assertion is supported, if support is needed, by his references to the futility and fatality of legalism (cf. Gal. 2:19; Rom. 7:7-25), by his statement that he advanced beyond all his contemporaries in the Jewish religion (Gal. 1:13-14), and by his claim that he was blameless with regard to the kind of righteousness that can come from legalistic practice (Phil. 3:6). Bornkamm thinks that Paul identified himself with the Jewish mission to the Gentiles, but on the stricter side which demanded circumcision of them. He sees the statement: "But if I, brethren, still preach circumcision, why am I still persecuted?" (Gal. 5:11) as evidence that Paul had at one time actually preached circumcision.[12] This may be true. The statement could also be interpreted as a false accusation based on Paul's having had Timothy circumcized.

Was Paul an apocalypticist? The answer is uncertain, but the evidence seems to indicate that he was, at least in a modified sense. This has often been denied because it was thought that he could not be a rabbi and be in the apocalyptic movement at the same time. Recent study has shown, however, that Judaism was a much more complex and complicated affair than was once thought. Apocalypticism seems to have been a movement which penetrated all strata of Jewish thought in the first century. The Dead Sea Scrolls have revealed a Jewish community which was highly legalistic and intensely eschatalogical in thought and practice.[13] Further, Paul, in common with other primitive Christians, used apocalyptic traditions to speak of the second advent of Jesus. This is self-evident from the epistles.[14] This does not mean that Paul brought Jewish apocalypticism over into Christianity unchanged. The character of his eschatology was determined by the significance which he saw in Jesus.[15] But apocalyptic traditions provided a suitable framework from which to preach the coming of Christ.

Persecutor of the church? Of course. His zeal for Judaism would naturally make him a persecutor. Christianity threatened the very foun-

THE JEW 15

dations of his religion as he saw it. Paul often spoke with shame of how he had persecuted the church (Phil. 3:6; Gal. 1:13). The grace of God was magnified in his eyes because God saved him and called him to apostleship in spite of this blot on his record: "For I am the least of the apostles, unfit to be called an apostle, because I persecuted the church of God. But by the grace of God I am what I am" (1 Cor. 15:9–10).

Acts tells of his persecution against the church in Jerusalem (Acts 8:3) which threatened to reach out to Damascus (Acts 22:5). Bornkamm challenges Acts on the basis of the statement that Paul was unknown by face to the churches of Judea (Gal. 1:22).[16] But this statement is insufficient grounds on which to deny the accuracy of Acts.

We see then that Paul, when he became a Christian, was a Jew. Behind him lay a lifetime of dedication to and zeal for the Jewish religion. Within him lay the heritage of the fathers. He did not renounce his Jewishness but boasted in it. He saw his new faith as the fulfillment of Judaism. Though he was unsparing in his condemnation of legalism, he never showed any symptoms of hostility to the Jews. Though he saw the inherent discontinuity between the Jewish and the Christian faith, he never saw them as antagonistic.

II. The Jewish Heritage in Paul's Christian Thought

Paul's thought was rooted in his Jewish heritage.[17] Albert Schweitzer opened the way for understanding Christianity, not in terms of opposition to Judaism, but in terms of fulfillment or finality.[18] The relationship of Paul to Judaism can no longer be "adequately expressed in terms of simple antitheses."[19]

This is true. Paul regarded his Christian proclamation as the fulfillment of the revelation of God to Israel. But some elements in his thought are more closely related to his Jewish heritage than others. His theology was not just the Jewish theology with Christ inserted. Much of it went far beyond that. Some of it was little more than that. Some of it was simply carrying over into his Christian life the ideas and thought patterns of the Jews.

1. Paul's Way of Thinking

Paul is often misunderstood by modern men, especially men of Western culture. We do not trouble to orient ourselves in the cultural and religious heritage of biblical writers. The dominating factor in that heritage was Jewish, not Greek. The dominating factor in our own cultural and religious heritage is Greek, not Jewish.

I recognize the danger of trying to set ways of thinking over against each other. The first-century world was a complex, synthetic world. There was a great deal of interaction and interweaving of cultural patterns. However, in broad outline, we may characterize, the Jewish way of thinking as functional and the Greek way of thinking as metaphysical.

The Jew asked, "What does it do?" The Greek, "What is it?" The Jew knew reality through what happened. The Greek sought to know reality by careful definition. For example, some insist that the doctrine of the trinity is a biblical doctrine. Nothing could be further from the truth. It is a fourth-century Greek-Christian formulation. No doubt, it is based on biblical data. No doubt, it was and is unsurpassed for what it is, an attempt to define the inner relationships of God.

This does not mean that Paul believed it or taught it. It attempts to answer questions which were utterly foreign to him. The question of the inner relation of God to himself never arose in his mind. He spoke of God, the Son, and the Holy Spirit. There is every reason to suppose that he attributed deity to all three. But he never asked how these manifestations of God were to be defined, one distinguishable from the other. His concern was for what God did, how man might come to experience his presence and power. He was engrossed with what it meant to walk in the Spirit, to be in union with Christ, and to worship the living God.

Far from separating these thoughts, he united them. He could say, "Now the Lord is the Spirit," thus identifying the Holy Spirit with Jesus Christ, the Son. In the same breath he added, "Where the Spirit of the Lord is, there is freedom," thus distinguishing one from the other (2 Cor. 3:17). If we attempt to interpret such language in our terms, it is nonsense, self-contradictory. But if we understand that Paul was speaking functionally, not metaphysically, it makes divine sense. He meant that an experience with the Lord (i.e., Jesus Christ) was an experience with the Holy Spirit. There is no way to distinguish one from the other, let alone to separate them. Yet, the Spirit's function in the world is to mediate the presence of the Lord. To that extent, the two can be distinguished. Paul believed, and this is orthodox Christianity, that his experience with God was rooted in the historical Christ-event, not in the realm of the purely spiritual.

Modern men are prone to inject their own conceptions into the Pauline material and thus misunderstand Paul. We need to be warned of this folly. Some are already aware of the danger and guard themselves against it. For others, the danger needs to be stressed. They have insisted on interpreting Paul as if he were a Greek. Our modern society is shifting, I think, back to the Jewish way of thinking. We can talk of atoms, but no one can define an atom. We can use electricity, but we cannot define it. Perhaps we will gradually align ourselves with Paul's way of thinking and, in the future, find it easier to understand him.

This is not to say that Paul's way of thinking was right and ours wrong. Each culture, each age has its own way of thinking, its own way of attempting to understand reality. Each is right for its own age and culture. Perhaps it is true that we must go on preaching and talking in the Greek way; we must if we hope to communicate to our own age. But if we want to understand Paul, we must understand him in the light of his own culture and age. His thought cannot be brought into our heritage without a radical reinterpretation of it, otherwise our interpretation will be a distortion.

2. Paul's Thought About God

We must remember that Paul knew God as the one who acts, who is steadfast in his love, who is present in the world and affairs of men. The Bible begins with the statement: "In the beginning God *created*" —acted to bring the world into existence. It does not begin with the statement: "In the beginning God existed." These first words of the Bible set the tone for the whole range of language about God in both the Old and New Testaments.

Compare these with modern attempts to speak about God. "God is the infinite and perfect Spirit in whom all things have their source, support, and end" (Strong). God is "a Spirit, infinite, eternal and unchangeable in his being, wisdom, power, holiness, justice, goodness and truth" (Westminster Confession). He is "the first cause and last end of all things" (Andrew Fuller).[20] What a different thought world! These statements may be true; they may have meaning to some minds. They have nothing to do with Paul. As a matter of fact, it may be doubted that any definition of God is of much value. A definition of God will be either too short to be comprehensive or too long to be practical.[21]

Turning to Paul's understanding of God, we note that what he says about God could (with few exceptions) be accepted by his Jewish contemporaries. This does not mean that his conversion and Christian experience gave him no new understanding of God; they did. It means that the difference was primarily one of stress and proportion rather than of basic content. This was true of Jesus; it was even more true of Paul.

(1) Paul believed in *the greatness and transcendence* of the living God. His majestic doxology can hardly be surpassed: "O the depth of the riches and wisdom and knowledge of God! How unsearchable are his judgments and how inscrutable his ways! 'For who has known the mind of the Lord, or who has been his counselor?' 'Or who has given a gift to him that he might be repaid?' For from him and through him and to him are all things. To him be glory forever. Amen." (Rom. 11:33–36).

Though Paul believed that all there was of God had been embodied in the earthly life of Jesus (Col. 2:9–10), this did not lead him to feel that God was a democratic God, that he had been lowered to our level. Again and again, he emphasized the majesty and greatness of his God. The Jewish confession, "God is one" was often repeated by Paul (cf. 1 Cor. 8:4,6; Gal. 3:20; Eph. 4:6; 1 Tim. 2:5). God, to Paul, was above all and through all and in all (Eph. 4:6). His invisible nature, that is, his eternal power and deity, are reflected but not exhausted in the world he made (Rom. 1:20; cf. Col. 1:15). The ultimate in sin is to fail to honor him as God and give him thanks (Rom. 1:21). It was unthinkable to Paul that men who had known the one, true God would be tempted to return to enslavement by weak and beggarly human elements (Gal. 4:8–9). God is the "King of ages, immortal, invisible, the only God" to whom belongs honor and glory for ever and ever (1Tim. 1:17; cf. Rom. 15:7; Eph. 3:21; Gal. 1:5).

(2) Along with his fellow Jews, Paul believed that *God was the righteous judge*. Before his court must all men appear and answer for their earthly deeds. The present plight of the Gentiles was the revelation of God's wrath against all those who suppress the truth (Rom. 1:18; cf. vv. 24–26,28). The exclusion of the Jewish people from redemption and their suffering at the hands of the Romans was a sign of God's wrath upon those who had received a revelation of God but had not conformed to it (1 Thess. 2:14–16; Rom. 2:3–4; 9:27–28; 11:8,21–22). So axiomatic is God's judgment that Gentile Christians dare not presume on their present blessings (Rom. 11:21–22) and the Christian apostle must work in its shadow (2 Cor. 5:11). The judgment of outsiders could be left in the hands of God who has said, "Vengeance is mine, I will repay" (Rom. 12:19; cf. 1 Cor. 5:13).

Some have taken Paul's statements on judgment *now* as an indication that Paul did not believe in the reality of God's wrath. Dodd sees Paul's presentation (i.e., in Rom. 1:18–32) as the presentation of a "natural process of cause and effect, and not as the direct act of God."[22] He seems to infer that Paul only retained the language of the Jews but modified

THE JEW

the concept of the wrath of God. This is not Paul's thought. Paul looked upon God as active in the whole process of judgment. The wrath of God he could understand; men deserved that. The love of God was the great paradox. That a righteous God could justify sinners was the unbelievable reality. The modern reluctance to admit that God may exercise wrath against sinners is a sign of how much we have been brainwashed by some interpreters of the Christian gospel and at the same time of how little we understand it.

This is not to say that God hates sinners. There is a difference between hate (in the modern sense) and wrath. Wrath is the refusal to manifest love; hatred is the refusal to cherish love. God certainly cherishes love for all men just as an angry father continues to cherish love for his disobedient child. The wrath of God is his "holy displeasure with evil, his fierce indignation against all impiety and immorality." As such it is only an expression of an attitude and action that could not be absent in a righteous God.[23]

Paul believed in the judgment of God *now;* he also believed in the future judgment of God. He warned his fellow Jews that by their hard and impenitent hearts they were storing up wrath for themselves "on the day of wrath when God's righteous judgment will be revealed. For he will render to every man according to his works" (Rom. 2:5–6). He asserted that all men will stand before the "judgment seat of God . . . so each of us shall give an account of himself to God" (Rom. 14:10–12).

(3) Paul believed in *the righteousness of God.* God, he thought, was self-consistent in all that he did.[24] This was so axiomatic to him that he could measure his own faithfulness and honesty by it (2 Cor. 1:18; Gal. 1:20). Even though the promises of God seem to have been nullified by the disobedience of Israel, the faithfulness of God was not to be questioned (Rom. 3:1–7; 9:6,14–16). The judgments of God are always righteous; he shows no partiality (Rom. 2:11). Both the perverse Gentile (Rom. 1:32) and the superficial Jew (Rom. 2:2) fall under his condemnation.

God's law is good because the giver of it is righteous. It does not bring salvation, but its weakness is not a reproach to God, but a sign of man's utter sinfulness (Rom. 7:22–25; 8:3–4). Because God is righteous, his people must be righteous also. Men who persist in sin can never be acceptable to God (Eph. 5:6). The church must have no partnership with heathen temples (2 Cor. 6:16) but must drive out from its midst all that defiles it (1 Cor. 5:3–8).

The Christian is to understand that he has been called to "holiness"

(1 Thess. 4:7–8) and that God's purpose is his complete sanctification (1 Thess. 5:23). Even life in slavery does not excuse one; a Christian slave's life is to be ruled by the thought of the righteousness of God (1 Tim. 6:1). The man of God is to cleanse himself of every defilement and make "holiness perfect in the fear of God" (2 Cor. 7:1). Imitating God, he must live in love (Eph. 5:1–2) and put on the "new nature, created after the likeness of God in true righteousness and holiness" (Eph. 4:24). A bishop, since he is God's steward, must be blameless and avoid any tendency to sin (1 Tim. 3:1–2). He must renounce underhanded methods and cunning speech (2 Cor. 4:2).

To Paul, righteousness is the very nature of God's being. He is not only "free from all evil, he is opposed to all evil." [25] Three consequences are seen: (a) God's righteousness demands that men be righteous; (b) it condemns sin in man; and (c) it moves God to redeem man from sin.[26] Each emphasis is found in the Old Testament, but the stress in Paul lies on the third consequence, that is, that God as righteous redeems man from sin. This is God's favorite way of opposing evil, of destroying it.

(4) That *God was the creator* of all things is axiomatic to Paul, the Christian, as it was to Paul, the Jew. To him, it was God who said, "Let light shine out of darkness" (2 Cor. 4:6). He is the source of all things (1 Cor. 8:6) and gives life to all living things (1 Tim. 6:13). The universe he made reveals his invisible nature and glory (Rom. 1:19–21). He gives each plant its own body (1 Cor. 15:38) and arranged the various parts of the human body as they exist (1 Cor. 12:18,24). He supplies our needs through seedtime and harvest (2 Cor. 9:10), and man may receive all that he made with thanksgiving (1 Tim. 4:3–5).

Paul is not so much making a point of God as the creator. He is using his belief in creation as an axiomatic assumption from which other consequences can be drawn. As with the Jews, creation is not an attempt to explain the universe but to show its relativity under the sovereign hand of God.

(5) To Paul, *God was the merciful God.* In talking of the grace of God, Paul was not discovering a new point of view. "In reality Paul was only expressing in his own words an old Jewish doctrine." [27] Paul's prayers of benediction and petition which he offers for his churches are filled with the belief that God is a God of mercy, grace, and love, one who gives peace to men. God is the one who comforts the downcast (2 Cor. 7:6). His own ministry is a signal evidence of God's mercy (2 Cor. 4:1). Even the judgments of God on Israel have the ultimate purpose of bestowing mercy upon them and all men (Rom. 11:32). God makes no distinction

between Jew and Greek but is merciful to all who call upon him (Rom. 9:12–13).

(6) Paul believed that *God controlled history for redemptive ends.* He received this basic concept from his Jewish heritage. Biblical theology is primarily a "recital" of God's mighty acts rather than a study of its ideas.[28] Its history is a history of God's acts rather than a study of evolving concepts.[29] "Salvation history" (Ger. *Heilsgeschichte*) is to some a catchword around which all biblical theology can be organized.[30] This is a valid perspective though it has been overemphasized by some. Its roots are in the Jewish way of thinking of God as acting in history to accomplish his purpose.

It may be doubted that Paul had a well-conceived salvation history in the sense of "an historical unfolding of a divine plan." [31] He did have a modified salvation-history perspective. He thought of the coming of Christ as the fulfillment of the ages (Gal. 4:4–5). He did speak of the epochs of Adam, Abraham, Moses, and Christ; this is thinking in terms of salvation history.[32] Paul went that far, but his gospel is more than a message of world mision. It is also, and perhaps basically, a message of individual salvation. There is no contradiction between the two emphases; we must simply beware of emphasizing the one to the exclusion of the other.

Paul certainly believed the purpose of God was the foundation of all that happened for the salvation of man. He applied this both to individual salvation (Rom. 8:28–30) and to the course of God's action in history (Rom. 9—11; Gal. 3:15 to 4:7). His gospel was a wisdom "which God decreed before the ages for our glorification" (1 Cor. 2:7).

Paul saw creation as the beginning of salvation history and looked upon the fall of man as creating the need for redemption (Rom. 1:19–21). He saw the call of Abraham and the promise that all the world would be blessed in him as the great continental divide of the past (Rom. 4:13; Gal. 3:6–8,16). The giving of the law was a temporary expedient, not meant to bring salvation, but meant to shut men up unto the salvation that was to be (Gal. 3:17–19). He looked on Israel as the chosen people of God whose choice was by grace, unto service, and was now fulfilled in the Christian movement (Rom. 4:11; 9:4–5,8,25–26; 11:1–2; Gal. 3:23).

3. *Paul's Conception of Man*

Paul's conception of man was completely Jewish.[33] Consequently it is completely foreign to modern thinking. No one will ever understand

Paul if he insists on making his language about man conform to Western thinking. There are three major differences.

One, Paul never thought of man himself in relation to man. His thought of man was always of man in his relationship to God. Like all Hebrew thinking about man, his was done in the vertical relation of man as God's creature.[34] So close is this relation that one could almost say that any statement which Paul makes about man is also a statement about God and, conversely, that any statement he makes about God is a statement about man.[35]

Two, Paul always thought of man as a member of the human race. Though he is concerned about the individual man and his salvation, he knows nothing of man in isolation from other men. For instance, in his use of "body," he sees the body as that which binds man to the rest of creation. It joins us to all people, without respect of individual or racial differences. Man is in life's bundle together with other men.[36] It is therefore not permissible, when interpreting Paul, to interpret man as "separable from the rest of the world."[37]

Three, Paul never spoke of man except to speak of him as a whole person. It is here that our Western way of thinking is most completely different from Paul. The Greeks, our cultural forebears, thought of man as a composite being, composed of complementary parts. Thus, man was body *plus* soul *plus* spirit. The spirit (or soul) of man was considered to be a spark of the divine imprisoned in the body which was essentially evil and temporal. The spiritual self was the essential self, incarcerated in a frame of matter, a kind of "angel in a slot machine."[38] Death, it was hoped, would release the soul from its prison to rejoin the divine substance from which it sprang. Talk of a bodily resurrection, to the Greek, was nonsense and repugnant. Resurrection would only be reimprisonment of the essential man.

For Paul, on the other hand, man was a unity. He always spoke of man as a total person. Any of many terms could be used to speak of the whole man, depending on what aspect or phase of human life was to be stressed. Thus, for Paul, body *equals* self; flesh *equals* self; spirit *equals* self; heart *equals* self; and, soul *equals* self. For him, such distinctions as "physical death" and "spiritual death" had no meaning. His teaching may permit us to speak in such terms; we must never accuse him of doing so. *Each term he uses speaks of the whole man.* This is our most important lesson to learn if we hope to understand Paul's language about man.

Why then the variety of terms? Paul used many: body, spirit, flesh, soul, heart, mind, consciousness, the outer man, the inner man, the old man, the new man, to mention the most common. When he used each term, he meant the whole man, but he meant man in some particular aspect of his being and existence.

This does not mean that he had a technical vocabulary with distinct and separate meanings for each word. It does mean that, in a general way, we can discern (and then let the context modify) what he meant by each term. What follows is an attempt to define some of his terms for man in this way. Caution is indicated in this quest. Scholars have debated long and loudly about the meaning of Paul's terms for man, each scholar seeming to be able to support his view from Paul's letters.[39] This would mean that different connotations are to be found in Paul and the context must remain all-important in interpreting him.

"Flesh" is used to mean the whole man as distinguished from God at two points—his finiteness and his sinfulness. The first contrast is common to the Old Testament and other New Testament writers. The second is peculiar to Paul. Paul uses the term ninety-one times, nearly half of which are found in Romans (twenty-six) and Galatians (eighteen) where the debate with the Judaizers is most prominent.

(1) About half (forty-seven) of these passages use "flesh" to stand for man as a human being—finite, weak—in contrast to God who is powerful, infinite, and divine. In these passages, flesh is not considered a *part* of the body, rather, it is the whole person "considered from the point of view of his external, physical existence."[40] Paul can speak of "infirmity in the flesh" (Gal. 4:13, KJV), "a thorn in the flesh" (2 Cor. 12:7, KJV), or "tribulation in the flesh" (1 Cor. 7:28). He can draw a contrast between the Jew who is a Jew only outwardly with a circumcision which is of the flesh, and the Jew who is one inwardly and whose circumcision is that of "the heart, in the spirit" (Rom. 2:28–29, KJV). Paul could be absent "in the flesh" but present "in the spirit" (Col.2:5, KJV). Within this use, flesh is not thought of as sinful and hostile to God in any way. Christ himself can be said to have been born of the seed of David "according to the flesh." (Rom. 1:3).[41] In this sense, flesh always, for Paul, has two inherent qualities—infirmity or weakness and mortality. The basis of comparison is always with God.[42]

(2) In about half (thirty-eight) of Paul's uses of *flesh,* the term seems to have overtones of sinfulness. This is not, however, because flesh is evil or impure within itself, but because "living according to the flesh" was a fundamental distortion of man's relationship with God. One could say that "flesh" is neutral in meaning when it means living *in* the world, but sinful in meaning when it means living *for* the world. When one does

this, he becomes a "man of the world by allowing his being-in-the-world . . . to govern his whole life and conduct." Thus Paul can speak of the flesh as striving against and opposing the Spirit of God (Rom. 8:4–6,9,13; Gal. 3:3; 4:26; 5:16–17,19). He can speak of the flesh being destroyed so that the spirit can be saved (1 Cor. 5:5). He can speak of flesh as the seat and instrument of sin (Rom. 7:5,18; 8:3; Gal. 5:13,24). What is in mind when Paul speaks thus of man as flesh is that man has denied his dependence on God and trusted in what is of human effort and origin.[44]

"Body" is another term which Paul uses often (ninety-one times). The body, for Paul, is the whole man.[45] Man does not *have* a body; he *is* a body.[46] The place where God meets me is, according to Paul, not the soul, but the body. Paul never used "body" to refer to a corpse as the Greeks did; he always used it for man as a living being in the world.

A case in point is Paul's discussion of the destructive power of sexual immorality (1 Cor. 6:13–20). Against libertines, Paul insisted that the body was spiritually meaningful. The body is meant for the Lord and the Lord is for the body (v. 13). Hence, the body should not be joined to a prostitute (v. 15). This leads to a union of the whole man with the prostitute. The man who does this sins against his own body (i.e., his own self). The body is "the temple of the Holy Spirit. . . . You are not your own; you were bought with a price. So glorify God in your body" (vv. 19–20). Throughout the passage, body equals self; "your body" is interchangeable with "yourself." Not only so, but the body is where God meets man. It is the sphere of faith and worship.[47] Christian worship is described by Paul as presenting "your bodies as a living sacrifice . . . to God" (Rom. 12:1). He meant, yourself as you exist in the world.

With this fundamental thought in mind, we may look at various ways in which Paul uses the term "body." In many passages, there is little if anything to distinguish between the use of *body* and *flesh*. Body, too, may be used to denote the outward, external man (Rom. 4:19; 1 Cor. 7:4; 1 Cor. 12:25; 13:3; 15:37–44). But there are notable areas of contrast. While the body may be enslaved by sin, it is never the seat of sin as flesh is (Rom. 6:6,12; 7:24; 8:10,13). The body is the area of Christian worship and praise. Paul could say, "glorify God in your body" (1 Cor. 6:20); he never said "glorify God in your flesh." Paul speaks of the body of Christ (Rom. 7:4; Col. 1:22) and sees the bread in the Lord's Supper as remembrance of his body (1 Cor. 11:24,27,29). He does not, nor could he, I think, use flesh in this way. He could speak of the resurrection of the body (Rom. 8:11,23; 1 Cor. 15:35–44; Phil. 3:21), but not of the flesh. He could call the church the body of Christ (Rom. 12:5; 1 Cor. 12:

12-13,27), but not the flesh of Christ. In these ways, when the context indicates, the use of *body* must be distinguished from the use of *flesh*.

"Spirit" is another synonym of Paul's for self and can take the place of the personal pronoun (1 Cor. 16:18).[48] Paul distinguishes between the spirit, as man, and the Holy Spirit (1 Cor. 2:11; Rom. 8:16).[49] When Paul uses "spirit," he is not thinking of some higher principle within man but of man himself.[50] Man does not, for Paul, consist of two parts nor three; he is a living unity. Spirit describes man as having a capacity for God and able to transmit his life (Rom. 8:16; 1 Cor. 2:10).

"Heart" is another anthropological term of Paul's. He never uses the word in the medical sense for the pump that circulates the blood in the human body (the circulation of blood was unknown in Paul's day). His use of this term comes close to modern use when "heart" is used figuratively for man's deepest feelings, emotions, desires, and purposes. For Paul, too, the heart is the center of thought, will, and feeling (1 Cor. 4:5).[51] Like all the other terms, heart "is a man's self, and in most cases where it is used it performs the service of a personal pronoun." [52]

Other terms could be discussed, but these are sufficient to indicate the direction of Paul's thought about man. We must remember that Paul thinks of man as related to God, as a part of the human race, and as a unity.

4. Paul's Use of the Old Testament

The chief advantage that the Jew had over the Gentile was that the Jews were "entrusted with the oracles of God" (Rom. 3:2). When Paul became a Christian, he did not throw away his Old Testament; he used it.[53] He did not lay aside as useless all the knowledge he had of the Old Testament in his Jewish life; "rather did he baptize it in Christ." [54]

Grobel suggests that the Old Testament is quoted 150 times in the New, often without any argumentative intent.[55] If Grobel's figures are correct, Paul quoted the Old Testament more than all other New Testament writers. He quoted the Old Testament directly 117 times in his letters.[56] Only Colossians and Titus have no quotations from the Old Testament.

Further, there are hundreds of allusions, often consisting of little more than the use of Old Testament phraseology. Moreover, there is frequent use of Old Testament analogies. Adam, Moses, David, and Abraham are quite at home in the Pauline house of thought. All of this means that Paul's thought was saturated in the Old Testament as it had come to be interpreted by Judaism.

In his use of the Old Testament, Paul showed himself to be a child of his time. His methods were rabbinical throughout. He was not averse to an allegorical interpretation of an Old Testament story (Gal. 4:21–31), though there is only one instance of this common practice of the rabbis.

Another notable example of his exegesis is: "Now to Abraham and his seed were the promises made. He saith not, And to seeds, as of many; but as of one, And to thy seed, which is Christ" (Gal. 3:16, KJV). The exegesis hangs upon the singular and plural of the word, *seed*. In Greek, the word has both a singular and a plural. Paul ignores the fact that the word in the original was collective, though singular. In Genesis 12:7, there can be no doubt that the promise contemplates all the descendants of Abraham.[57] Paul thus lifts the passage out of its context, lays hold of the singular form of the noun, and connects the promise with Christ.

Further study shows that Paul makes use of other rabbinical methods. His quotations were taken largely from the Greek Old Testament, but thirty-eight of them differ from both the Greek translation and the Hebrew original.[58] In many cases, it turns out that Paul has paraphrased the passage and made his own translation. This is the use of what is known as *pesher* (i.e., interpretive paraphrase), which was common among the rabbis and is found often in the Dead Sea Scrolls.[59]

These examples show how faulty Paul's exegesis was. However, we must not judge him by modern standards. He was proclaiming what he thought was the true meaning of the Scripture.[60] He was not attempting to deceive, but was citing the Old Testament as it was commonly understood in his day to support the Christian gospel.

But, in Paul's case, faulty methods did not lead to faulty doctrine. We need not renounce his gospel because we cannot accept his exegesis. You see, his doctrine *was not based* on the Old Testament. There is no evidence that he ever derived any Christian teaching from the Old Testament. Rather, his doctrine came from the teaching and example of Jesus or from his own Spirit-led experience and judgment.[61] It is therefore somewhat misleading to say that the Old Testament was Paul's Bible. It was and yet it wasn't. It is true that the Old Testament was the only written Scriptures which he regarded as inspired of God. It was not true that he derived his doctrines from the exegesis of the Old Testament as modern Christians derive theirs by exegesis of the New Testament. Paul buttressed and supported his thought, received by revelation, by appeal to the Old Testament. At other times, he merely expressed the truth he wished to communicate in the words and phraseology of the Old Testament. The validity of his thought must rest upon the reality of God's revelation to him. When judged at this bar, Paul stands vindicated.

We see that Paul was first of all and always (though not always first of all) a Jew. It is (as is apparent from my discussion) impossible to separate his thinking into distinct strata and trace each particular element to its source. Paul wrote as a Christian missionary. If he had written as a Jew and we had what he wrote, the story would be plainer. It is evident that much of his thought was rooted in Jewish thinking. This is true even if it did not stop there. It seems to me that the aspects of his thought which we have discussed here are most clearly related to his Jewish heritage. If so, some understanding of that heritage is essential to our understanding Paul.

NOTES

1. W. D. Davis, *Paul and Rabbinic Judaism* (London: S.P.C.K., 1955) p. 324.
2. *Ibid.*, p. 321.
3. A. C. Purdy, "Paul the Apostle," *Interpreter's Dictionary of the Bible* (Nashville: Abingdon Press, 1962) Vol. 3, p. 688.
4. Davies, *op. cit.*, p. 323.
5. William Barclay, *The Mind of St. Paul* (New York: Harper, 1958) p. 14.
6. *Ibid.*, p. 12.   7. *Ibid.*
8. Cf. T. W. Manson, *On Paul and John* (London: SCM Press, 1963), p. 12.
9. Purdy, *op. cit.*, p. 689.
10. Gunther Bornkamm, *Paul* (New York: Harper & Row, publishers, 1971), p. 11.
11. Davies, *op. cit.*, p. 16.   12. *Op. cit.*, p. 12.
13. Davies, *op. cit.*, p. xi.   14. *Ibid.*, pp. 286–7.
15. *Ibid.*, p. 290.   16. *Op. cit.*, p. 15.
17. Cf. Davies, *op. cit.*   18. *Ibid.*, p. xiii.
19. *Ibid.*, p. xv.
20. A. H. Strong, *Systematic Theology* (Philadelphia: Judson Press, c. 1907), p. 52.
21. W. T. Conner, *Revelation and God* (Nashville: Broadman Press, 1936), p. 211.
22. C. H. Dodd, *The Epistle of Paul to the Romans* (New York: Harper & Row, n.d.), p. 29.
23. Willibald Beyschlag, *New Testament Theology* (Edinburgh: T. & T. Clark, 1895), pp. 92–3.
24. W. T. Conner, *The Faith of the New Testament* (Nashville: Broadman Press, 1940), p. 273.
25. W. T. Conner, *Revelation and God*, p. 247.
26. *Ibid.*, pp. 248–252.
27. H. J. Schoeps, *Paul* (Philadelphia: Westminster Press, 1961), p. 206.
28. G. Ernest Wright, *God Who Acts* (Chicago: Henry Regnery Co., 1953), p. 32.
29. *Ibid.*, p. 38.
30. Cf. Oscar Cullmann, *Salvation in History* (London: SCM Press, 1967).
31. *Ibid.*, p. 249.
32. Ernst Käsemann, *Perspectives on Paul* (Philadelphia: Fortress Press, c. 1971), p. 65.
33. John A. T. Robinson, *The Body* (London: SCM Press, 1952), p. 11.
34. *Ibid.*, pp. 15–16.   35. Käsemann, *op. cit.*, p. 1.
36. Robinson, *op. cit.*, p. 29.   37. Käsemann, *op. cit.*, p. 15.
38. Robinson, *op. cit.*, p. 12.
39. Cf. Robert Jewett, *Paul's Anthropological Terms* (Leiden: E. J. Brill, 1971), p. 1.
40. Robinson, *op. cit.*, p. 17–18.   41. Eduard Schweizer, *sarx* (TDNT), VII, p. 125.
42. Robinson, *op. cit.*, p. 20.   43. *Ibid.*, p. 25.
44. *Ibid.*
45. *Ibid.*, p. 28. Schweizer, *soma*, (TDNT), VII, p. 1065.

46. Hans Conzelmann, *An Outline of the Theology of the New Testament* (New York: Harper & Row, Publishers, c. 1969), p. 176.
47. Schweizer, *soma*, (TDNT), VII, p. 1066.
48. Rudolf Bultmann, *Theology of the New Testament* (New York: Charles Scribner's Sons, 1951), Vol. I., p. 206.
49. Conzelmann, *op. cit.*, p. 180.   50. Bultmann, *op. cit.*, p. 206.
51. Conzelmann, *op. cit.*, p. 181 and Jewett, *op. cit.*, p. 448.
52. Bultmann, *op. cit.*, p. 220.   53. Barclay, *Mind of St. Paul*, p. 15.
54. R. V. G. Tasker, *The Old Testament in the New Testament* (Grand Rapids, Mich.: Wm. B. Eerdmans Publishing Co., c. 1954), p. 84.
55. K. Grobel, "Quotations," IDB 3:977.
56. Cf. Tables of *The Greek New Testament* ed. by Kurt Aland, Matthew Black, Bruce M. Metzger, and Allen Wikgren (London: United Bible Societies, 1966), pp. 897–920.
57. H. E. Dana and R. E. Glaze, Jr., *Interpreting the New Testament* (Nashville: Broadman Press, 1961), p. 52.
58. E. Earle Ellis, "A Note on Pauline Hermeneutics," *New Testament Studies,* Nov. 1955, p. 127.
59. *Ibid.*   60. *Ibid.*, p. 132.
61. Charles Buck and Greer Taylor, *Saint Paul* (Charles Scribner's Sons, 1969), p. 61.

2
THE CONVERT

The Jew became the convert; the persecutor became the promotor; the menace became the missionary. The proud Pharisee became Christ's slave. The conversion of Paul became the watershed of his life, the eschatological event that made him what he became.

I. "He Appeared to Me"

Paul listed himself among those who were eyewitnesses to the resurrection (1 Cor. 15:8). When opponents challenged his apostolic credentials, he asked, "Have I not seen the Jesus our Lord?" (1 Cor. 9:1). "He met Christ. . . . Of that he was certain. . . . It revolutionized his life." [1] To Paul, his conversion was not so much an experience as it was an event, an event when Christ was revealed to him in his true essence.

Our knowledge of that event is limited. Three accounts of the Damascus Road event appear in Acts (9:1–19; 22:4–16; 26:9–18). He, himself, mentions his conversion in several passages (Gal. 1:15–16; 2:19–21; 6:14; Phil. 3:7–11,12; Titus 3:3; the two passages in 1 Corinthians mentioned above, and possibly elsewhere). Some think that the vision he describes (2 Cor. 12:2–5) is an account of his conversion.[2] This is challenged by most students of Paul's life. Paul had and told of other visions and revelations (Gal. 2:1; Acts 18:9; 22:17; 23:11). But he made a sharp distinction between these and "seeing" the Lord. Concerning his visions, he is hesitant to speak, regarding them as private and thinking that to speak of them would be "boasting." [3] A study of the passages cited will indicate some elements in his conversion which are important.

1. It Was on God's Initiative

Paul speaks of it as being "called through [the] grace" of God who "was pleased to reveal his Son to me" (Gal. 1:15–16). He speaks of it as being "apprehended," i.e., laid hold of by Christ (Phil. 3:12). He speaks of it as an "appearance" of the "kindness of God our Savior"

(Titus 3:3). Nothing short of this kind of divine intervention in his life could be an "accurate description of his conversion." [4] He was conscious of having been "conquered by a power beyond his own self," arrested by God himself.[5]

2. It Involved a Decision on Paul's Part

Paul's conversion was no overcoming of his own will; he saw it as having involved a decision which he himself made. Confronted with the living Christ, he "counted as loss" whatever advantage he had had as a Jew (Phil. 3:7). He "died" (Gal. 2:19) that day, being "crucified with Christ" (Gal. 2:20) and the "world" died to him as well (Gal. 6:14). He was a willing captor.

Anyone who is saved is conscious that his salvation is wholly and entirely the work of God, but he is also conscious that his salvation came as a result of a definite decision on his own part. Thus, it was with Paul. When speaking of his conversion, he sometimes used language that would seem to eliminate human choice entirely and make it completely and utterly an act of God. At other times, he used language which would seem to make it completely and utterly his own decision.

3. Did God Use Human Means to Capture Paul?

Some would insist that Paul's experience came to him without "psychological preparation of any kind." [6] Usually this conclusion is based on the assumption that if the conversion was a revelation, an act of God, it could have no human preparation. This assumption, however, is unfounded on fact. The use of human means does not make the act of God any less the act of God. In Paul's case, three human factors are present.

One, Paul was not satisfied with his Judaism. Bultmann insists that Paul's conversion was not the result of "an inner moral collapse" or "a rescue from despair." [7] With this opinion, many modern scholars agree. No doubt, such opinions are a reaction to former attempts to overemphasize the psychological aspects of Paul's conversion. But the correction is, I think, an over-correction.

I cannot avoid the feeling that Paul's description of the futile struggle to win the approval of God through legalism reflects, in some degree, his own pre-Christian struggles (Rom. 7:7–25). There is a poignancy about this chapter which speaks of a personal involvement. Of course, Paul is speaking from the perspective of his Christian experience, and it would be wrong to say that, as a Jew, he felt as deeply as the chapter indicates. Listen to his words: "When the commandment came, sin revived and I died" (v. 9). "Did that which is good, then bring death to me? By no means! It was sin, working death in me through what is good, in order that sin might be shown to be sin, and through the commandment might become sinful beyond measure" (v. 13). "Wretched man that I am! Who will deliver me from this body of death?" (v. 24).

This whole chapter yields a picture of a man caught up in the reality of sin, struggling against it, seeking to overcome it by keeping the law and finally coming to despair. Even though the description is retrospective, it seems to be quite personal. The proud Pharisee was, deep down in his heart, struggling with a sense of his own inadequacy and seeking a way of victory which he found only when he found Christ.

Two, Paul had had contact with the early Christian community. He had heard their preaching; this is why he became a persecutor.[8] Bultmann even asserts that Paul was "won to the Christian faith by the kerygma of the Hellenistic Church."[9] No doubt, Bultmann goes too far. It was not this preaching alone which led to his conversion, but it must have been a factor in it.

Contact with the church was also contact with Christ who was the center of the persecuted community. Through that contact, Christ began "to make himself known to Paul."[10] If we can trust the Acts account, Paul may have entered into active debate with Stephen concerning the messiahship of Christ—and lost! "Then some of those who belonged to the synagogue . . . of those from Cilicia and Asia [Was this Paul's Jerusalem synagogue? Likely it was.], arose and disputed with Stephen. But they could not withstand the wisdom and the Spirit with which he spoke" (Acts 6:9–10). Stephen lost his life as a result of his skill as a debater. But before he did, he made a magnificent defense of his gospel before the Jewish court, and Paul was no doubt there. In other words, Paul had heard the gospel; he had not been able to refute it. Could there have been nagging doubts in his mind that it might be the truth? Probably.

Three, Paul saw a Christian martyr die in such a way as he would have liked to be able to die. They had laid the garments of Stephen down at the feet of young Saul (Acts 7:58) and he was "consenting to his death" (Acts 8:1). He had heard the condemned man say as he gazed into heaven, "Behold, I see the heavens opened, and the Son of man standing at the right hand of God" (Acts 7:56). He had heard him pray for his tormentors (Acts 7:60) and die with the peaceful prayer, "Lord Jesus, receive my spirit" (Acts 7:59). Could Paul have been untouched by what he saw? Perhaps; other Jews seem to have been. But if our analysis of his inner struggles against fear and nagging doubts about the gospel are true, the death of Stephen could have been nothing less than a traumatic experience to Paul. It is reasonable, therefore, to suppose that Paul did have some psychological preparation for the revelation of Christ which God made to him on the Damascus Road.

4. Was Paul's Conversion a Pattern or Exception?

It is quite common to suppose that Paul's experience represents a once-for-all-time experience like the creation of the world. Other Christians, it is supposed, have a different kind of conversion experience. Paul did not think so. He thought of his conversion as the normative pattern of Christian conversion. "He never speaks of himself as being 'in Christ' in any way" which is unlike the experience of every other believer.[11]

Of course, others were not saved on their way to persecute the church, nor did they see a blinding light and have a vision of the risen Christ. But this was not the essence of his conversion as Paul saw it.

The essence of his experience was a realization of his own sinfulness and unworthiness and the reception of the unmerited favor of God. When he describes the conversion of the Gentiles, he takes his place with them and says: "We ourselves were once foolish, disobedient, led astray, slaves to various passions and pleasures, passing our days in malice and envy, hated by men [rather, hateful to men] and hating one another" (Titus 3:3). He reminds Peter that though he and Peter were not "Gentile sinners" yet "we ourselves also were found to be sinners" and this was essential to their conversion; it was "in order to be justified by faith in Christ" (Gal. 2:15–17).

That the God who saved Paul through faith must also save others in the same way is indicated by: "For by grace you have been saved through faith . . . for we are his workmanship, created in Christ Jesus" (Eph. 2:8,10). Paul saw others, as well as himself, as the handiwork of God's grace. In this there could be no distinction.

James Stewart[12] debates the question of the typicalness of Paul's conversion with Johannes Weiss.[13] Weiss points out the many ways in which the normal modern Christian's background and experience differs from that of Paul. Stewart admits the superficial differences but points out that no man can save himself. It is this which makes "Paul's Gospel universally cogent, for it is the burden of everything he has to say."[14] The real antithesis, he says, is not between those who have been saved in one way and those who have been saved by another way. It is between those who "have personally committed their lives to God, and those who have not." [15] I agree with Stewart.

5. Paul's New Self-understanding

That Paul's conversion resulted in a new self-understanding, there can be no doubt. I doubt if we can say that the whole of his conversion was simply the acceptance "of God's judgment upon his self-understanding up to that time." [16] But there can be little doubt that his conversion was the "changing point" in his whole life and created a new "center of his life." [17] What this change amounted to will be seen in his theology and its development, for his theology has been characterized as a "conversion-theology."

However, we can take note here of two motifs which characterize Paul's self-understanding following his conversion. One, he regarded himself as the slave of Jesus Christ (Rom. 1:1; Gal. 1:10; Phil. 1:1; cf. also Rom. 6:14–23 which demands that Christians yield themselves to God as instruments of righteousness). Taking hold of the common relation of slave and master, he cast himself in the role of the slave. The lordship of Christ, to him, was a living reality. Before his conversion, Paul had been the center of his own world; after it, Christ was the center. His conversion was from a "self-centered" life to a "Christ-centered" life.[18] No longer did he see himself as having the right of personal decision; Christ became the decision-maker in his life. But he did not regard slavery to Christ as repugnant. Paradoxically, he saw it as the achievement of real freedom. He saw himself as a slave to sin who had been liberated (Gal. 5:1) and spoke of "our freedom which we have in Christ" (Gal. 2:4) as a treasure to be guarded with one's life.

Two, Paul spoke of his present life in these words: "It is no longer I who live, but Christ who lives in me" (Gal 2:20). What he means by this will be discussed later under the term, "in Christ." Here, we note it only to indicate that it was a part of Paul's new self-understanding that ruled his life from this point on.

II. Theology Reorientated

Paul's conversion led to a new theology, rather to a shift of the center of gravity in his old theology. "Following his conversion, he saw everything with new eyes." [19] Speaking of the time immediately following his conversion, he said, "I did not confer with flesh and blood, nor did I go up to Jerusalem to those who were apostles before me, but I went away into Arabia; and again I returned to Damascus" (Gal. 1:16–17).

Paul did not tell us why he went away into Arabia (a wilderness place), but it is not hard to guess why. He went away to reflect on his beliefs. The experience with Christ on Damascus Road was a cataclysmic invasion not only of his inner self but of his theology. His new insight into the meaning of Jesus of Nazareth must be integrated into all that he had previously thought.

His conversion called for "a reorganization of his Jewish messianic faith and hope." [20] His conversion, more than most others, was a "theological conversion." [21] From now on, not only his spiritual life, but his theology must be centered in the meaning of Christ for him.[22]

How long did this rethinking last? We do not know. In one sense, it lasted to the end of his life. In its initial stage, we have his timetable in Galatians: Conversion—visit to Arabia—return to Damascus—first visit to Jerusalem (three years from first to last) (Gal. 1:16–18). But, we do not know how long the preaching in Damascus lasted and thus we cannot say with assurance how long Paul remained in Arabia. It was long enough. His theology, from now on, will be Christ centered and this must be said to be due to his conversion.

What needed revision? Everything. It is tempting to begin here and attempt to set out all of Paul's theology, but we must avoid the temptation. Other factors entered into his mature thought and we must give attention to them. However, some elements are basic and to these we now turn.

1. A New Conception of Jesus

The first and most revolutionary change in Paul's thought was with regard to Jesus. As a Jew, he had seen him as an imposter, a false Messiah who did not measure up to the Jewish expectations. He had debated the question with Stephen (perhaps) and tried to show that Jesus could not have been the expected Messiah. He had helped to kill Stephen and was now on his way to persecute all those of the hated sect who glorified Jesus.

Then he met the living Christ. He saw that he had been wrong. Jesus of Nazareth was the living Messiah, enthroned at the right hand of God. There could no longer be any doubt of that; God had revealed his Son to him.

Paul mentions this revolution in his thinking when he says: "From now on, therefore, we regard no one from a human point of view [i.e., according to the flesh]; even though we once regarded Christ from a human point of view, we regard him thus no longer" (2 Cor. 5:16). This verse, I think, refers to his new perspective gained at the time of his conversion. Before his conversion, Paul had judged the claims of Jesus "from a human point of view" and found him wanting. After his conversion, he regarded him from another viewpoint entirely, that is, from the Christian point of view. When looked at in this way, he was convinced that Jesus was indeed the Son of God, the fulfillment of the promises of God, the rightful Lord of all men. All that Paul later learned of Jesus, all of his later Christology, is rooted in his own conversion experience.[23]

To be more specific, there are at least three things about Jesus Christ that Paul learned from his experience.

(1) He lived. He who had died on an accursed cross was alive.[24] This fact must be rated as a miracle of the first order in the mind of Paul. The resurrection of Jesus became a cornerstone of his life and ministry.[25] Though the cross was the center of his gospel, it was never isolated from the resurrection. It was not the death of Christ which he later preached, but the living Christ who had been crucified (1 Cor. 2:1).

This meant that Paul was not converted to Christianity, he was converted to Christ. His conversion did not mean his acceptance of a formulation of faith; it meant the acceptance of Christ as the Anointed One of God.[26] The resurrection meant that Jesus was the rightful Lord of his life, and Paul was glad to yield him that allegiance that made him so in fact.

The fact that Christ was alive meant that he was no impious imposter; he belonged to God's realm of glory; he could be none other than the Messiah whom the Jews expected from heaven.[27]

(2) The conversion of Paul also meant a new assessment of the cross of Christ. Previously he had looked upon it as the final proof that Jesus could not have been the Messiah. The law pronounced a curse on those who died in this manner (Gal. 3:13). Later, Paul saw that Christ had borne the curse "for us" and redeemed us by it (Gal. 3:13–14). How much of a theology of the cross was revealed to Paul at the time of his conversion and how much came to him in later life, we do not know.

Certainly, he had to rethink the cross.[28] It had been the great stumbling block of the gospel to Paul as it became to other Jews (1 Cor. 1:23). The vision of the risen Christ meant that God had reversed the judgment of men. They condemned Jesus and put him to death; God raised him from the dead. This could mean nothing less than that men had made a mistake, a tragic blunder, in their judgment. It must mean God's condemnation of human wisdom and human attempts to win the approval of God through works. Later, the apostle would write concerning the "hidden wisdom of God": "None of the rulers of this age understood this; for if they had, they would not have crucified the Lord of glory" (1 Cor. 2:8).

2. A New Understanding of Salvation History

Paul, as a Jewish theologian, had learned that God is a God of action; he is known through what he does. Paul had learned to interpret the past as the story of God's action in the world. The stories of Adam, of Abraham, of Jacob, of Moses, of the judges and kings of Israel, of the prophets—these stories had been told and retold to thrill Paul's Jewish heart with their account of God's movement in history toward a definite purpose. As an apocalyptic Jew, Paul looked forward to the longed-for day when God would demonstrate his power and might in the destruction of the world, the judgment of all men, and the salvation of those who deserved justification.

All this had to be rethought in the light of the Damascus Road experience. It did not need to be discarded; it did need a radical reformulation. Christ lived; he was the Messiah. Yet the world still stood and the judgment had not happened. What was God about anyhow? Where had the Jewish theologians gone wrong?

First, they had gone wrong in supposing that God was moving toward judment as his primary goal. He was not; he was moving toward redemption. What he had seen proved that. The purpose of God was redemptive.

Second, they had gone wrong in supposing that redemption and judgment would be one event. Paul had to reorganize his thinking to allow for the fact that redemption had come, but final judgment had not. His salvation history had to be reformulated.[29]

What it amounted to now was that God had been acting in Adam, Abraham, Moses, and the rest of Old Testament history toward a climax of redemption which had now taken place in Christ Jesus. Jesus became the midpoint of salvation history with more yet to come. The end of the ages had come, but the end was not termination but goal. Later Paul could write, "Christ is the end of the law" (Rom. 10:4). By this, he meant that the law reached its goal in Christ.

3. A New Conception of God

Paul came to see God as he really is in the fact and person of the risen Christ. He learned that God's glory was not to be seen "in the stern visage of a judge, but in the face of Jesus Christ." Characteristic of his thought of God from now on was to be that he knew God "as the God

THE CONVERT

and Father of our Lord Jesus Christ" (Rom. 15:6; 2 Cor. 1:3; 9:31; Col. 1:3; Eph. 1:3).

Perhaps it is too much to say that this was a new conception of God. Paul's Jewish heritage had been more right at this point than any other. But his "center of gravity" was misplaced. The emphasis lay on the complete "otherness" of God, his transcendence. Stress was laid on God's righteousness, not as a redemptive quality, but as a quality of judgment.

Paul's conversion meant the radical transformation of his idea of God. Without sacrificing any aspect of his Jewish faith, he now saw that the center of gravity in one's thought about God must be his nearness, his mercy. While God was to be worshiped, he was not to be feared. His presence should induce awe but not terror. He was to be reverenced but not shunned. God had revealed himself in the person of Christ as the God of mercy and redemption.

4. A New Conception of Salvation

As a Jew, Paul had two fundamental ideas about salvation. One, salvation was a human achievement. God had given the law and pointed the way; it was up to man to become righteous by careful obedience to the law. His watchword was: "Moses writes that the man who practices the righteousness which is based on the law shall live by it" (Rom. 10:5). Two, salvation was to come at the end of time. Only at the final judgment would men know whether or not they had "made it." Life, in the meantime, must be lived in anxiety and fear. Any breach of the law meant condemnation; only by persistent and careful obedience could anyone hope at last to be vindicated by God.

Then Paul saw Jesus! Everything was changed. The living Christ spoke to him with tenderness and made him know that he was already accepted with God and forgiven for his sins.

This meant everything to Paul in his own experience; it changed a great deal in his theology. First, he saw that salvation was not man's achievement but God's gift of grace. No man could earn salvation; no man could achieve it for himself. Only God could be its author. All that Paul ever said later about the grace of God finds its root in his own conversion experience.

Second, Paul saw salvation as a present possession, an assured hope. No longer must man await the judgment to find out if he had "made it." He could know now, in Christ Jesus, that he had been accepted by God. Though more was yet to come; it was to be of the same order as that which had already come in his life.

5. *A New Conception of the Church*

As a Jew, Paul had looked upon the church in Jerusalem as his enemy; he had persecuted it and tried to destroy it. He looked upon its leaders as unlearned men who were little short of madmen. They were preaching a message that was utterly untrue.

Then he met Jesus. Jesus said, "Why do you persecute me?" (Acts 9:4). With these words, Jesus identified himself with the despised band in Jerusalem. Paul saw the church as a divine institution, embodying in itself the very life of God in Christ. From this point on, there would be no greater champion of the church and its ministry than Paul.

III. Paul and Jesus of Nazareth

For almost two centuries, scholars have attempted to drive a wedge between Paul and Jesus of Nazareth. In the nineteenth century the concern of many scholars was to save what they considered to be true Christianity. Paul was looked upon as one who had taken the mild and gentle rabbi, Jesus, and made a god out of him. Instead of continuing and perpetuating the teachings of Jesus, Paul had misled men into worshiping him as a heavenly being. In their minds, Paul had misinterpreted Christ and his theology bore no kinship to the earthly Jesus at all.

In the twentieth century, the same drive has continued, but from different motives. The greatest spokesman for those who would separate Paul from Jesus is Rudolf Bultmann.[30] He insists that Paul knew little of the earthly Jesus, only that he had lived and died. Bultmann believes that this was all that Paul was concerned about, that the life and words of Jesus had no theological relevance to Paul. Paul worshiped the living Christ; he cared nothing for the man of Nazareth.

Much of Bultmann's stand is based on an argument from silence. Since Paul did not fill his letters with quotations from the teachings of Jesus, since he did not recount the events in the earthly career of Jesus in his letters, Bultmann concludes that he knew nothing of these things and cared even less.

We must remember that Paul's letters were written to churches concerning pressing problems in the fellowships of the saints. He assumed the knowledge of Jesus and the Christian gospel which was common to all Christians in his day. The problems Paul faced were not the problems Jesus faced. The "words" of Jesus were not always relevant to the problems he sought to solve. This, rather than ignorance, would explain why there are so few references to the earthly Jesus in Paul's letters.

But what will explain why there are so many? If Paul knew nothing of Jesus and cared less, why did he ever quote his words or point to his example? He does both. And he does it in such a natural way that it would assume considerable knowledge of Jesus on the part of his converts. Four times in his epistles he refers to the words of "the Lord" by which he meant the teachings of the earthly Jesus (1 Cor. 7:10; 9:14; 11:23-25; 1 Thess. 4:15-17). In these instances, Paul was quick to cite the words of Jesus as the final authority concerning Christian problems. When the teachings of Jesus were relevant, they were used. Nor must we forget that Paul in two passages (Rom. 8:15; Gal. 4:6) calls God "Abba." In another connection, I have shown that this terminology goes back to Jesus of Nazareth.[31] There is no doubt in my mind that Paul knew of Jesus' use and copied it to express his own deepest devotion to God.

There are several passages in which Paul points to the example of Jesus' earthly life to enforce either his theology or the exhortation which he addresses to his readers. He uses the "meekness and gentleness" of Christ (2 Cor. 10:1) as the basis of appeal to the Corinthians. He speaks of the "obedience" of Christ (Rom. 5:19) as culminating in his sacrifical death. He speaks of the "steadfastness" of Christ (2 Thess. 3:5) as a virtue to be emulated by the Thessalonians. He speaks of the "grace" of Christ (2 Cor. 8:9) to encourage liberal giving by the Corinthians. He thought of himself as being "an imitator" of Christ (1 Cor. 11:1) and urged his converts to imitate him to the extent that he imitated Christ. He could hardly have talked about imitating Christ unless he had a living, concrete picture of the personality of Jesus.[32]

Of the events in the life of Jesus, Paul said little. Most of what he said is clustered around the cross. Of the closing scenes of Jesus' life, he seems to have been well informed. He knew that Jesus had instituted the Lord's Supper on the "night when he was betrayed" (1 Cor. 11:23). He calls Christ "our paschal lamb" (1 Cor. 5:7) which may indicate the exact date of Jesus' death. He knew that the Jews had brought about his death (1 Thess. 2:15). He knew the method of his death as a crucifixion (1 Cor. 2:8; Gal. 3:13).

From this data, it would appear that Paul both knew of the earthly life of Jesus and respected it. Of course, his message was not one of the Jesus of Nazareth; it was a message of the saving power of the living Christ. His task was not to perpetuate the teachings of Jesus but to challenge men to submit to the lordship of Christ. However, he seems not to have been ignorant of that life. From his ample relations with men (his fellow workers and Peter) who knew Jesus in his earthly life, he could have learned much about Jesus. The evidence seems to indicate that he made good use of his opportunities.[33]

NOTES

1. W. T. Conner, *Faith of the New Testament*, p. 259.
2. Buck and Taylor, *Saint Paul*, p. 222.
3. John Knox, *Chapters in the Life of Paul* (Nashville: Abingdon Press, 1950), p. 121.
4. Elias Andrews, *The Meaning of Christ for Paul* (Nashville: Abingdon-Cokesbury Press, 1949), p. 15.
5. Philippe H. Menoud, "Revelation and Tradition," *Interpretation*, April, 1953, p. 134.
6. Knox, *op. cit.*, p. 123.   7. *Theology*, V. I, p. 188.
8. Hans Conzelmann, *Outlines of New Testament Theology*, p. 163.
9. *Op. cit.*, p. 187.   10. Knox, *op. cit.*, p. 126.
11. *Ibid.*, p. 112.
12. *A Man in Christ* (New York: Harper and Brothers, n.d.), pp. 127-131.
13. *Das Urchristentum* (cited by Stewart, *op. cit.*).   14. Stewart, *op. cit.*, p. 130.
15. *Ibid.*, p. 131.   16. Bultmann, *Theology*, Vol. I, p. 187.
17. Conner, *Faith*, p. 259.   18. T. W. Manson, *On Paul and John*, pp. 13-14.
19. Paul Clasper, *New Life in Paul* (Lutterworth Press, 1961), p. 10.
20. Menoud, *op. cit.*, p. 131.   21. *Ibid.*
22. Conner, *Faith*, p. 259.
23. J. A. Fitzmeyer, S. J. *Pauline Theology* (New Jersey; Prentice, 1967), p. 8.
24. H. F. Rall, *According to Paul* (New York: Scribner's, 1950), p. 15.
25. H. G. Wood, "The Conversion of Paul," *New Testament Studies*, May, 1955, p. 281.
26. *Ibid.*, p. 281.   27. Rall, *op. cit.*, p. 15.
28. Wood, *op. cit.*, p. 279.   29. Fitzmeyer, *op. cit.*, p. 10.
30. Cf. *Theology*, Vol. 1, pp. 188-189, for a convenient summary of Bultmann's position.
31. Fred L. Fisher, *Jesus and His Teachings* (Nashville: Broadman Press, 1972), p. 90.
32. Hunter, *Predecessors*, p. 11.   33. *Ibid.*, p. 12.

3
THE CHRISTIAN

Paul learned much from his conversion, but he learned more from his fellow Christians. This may surprise you. It shouldn't. So much has been said about the creativity and originality of the apostle that some have thought he was a complete individualist who could not be assimilated into early Christian life.[1] It is true that Paul was a creative thinker, but his creativity and individuality have been greatly overstated.[2]

Paul thought of himself as "one in a succession,"[3] one who carried on the traditions of Jesus which had been handed on to him by those who went before him. In the best sense of the words, Paul was a traditionalist, a conformist, an adherent, an establishment man. He was not the founder of a new religion but an apostle of a faith "already preached before him." He had a high sense of historical continuity with the past.[4] He would have resented any implication that he was a "religious genius" whose theology was fashioned out of his own experiences.[5]

Of course, Paul did break new ground in his theology; he did preach the gospel in terms and with implications that went far beyond his religious heritage. His missionary endeavor forced him to go ahead, but he never departed from the heritage. His gospel was the one, common gospel of all Christians. The differences which are discernible were more a matter of terminology and scope than of essence.

I. Paul's Respect for His Predecessors

"For I would have you know, brethren, that the gospel which was preached by me is not man's gospel. For I did not receive it from man, nor was I taught it, but it came through a revelation of Jesus Christ" (Gal. 1:11,12). These words are easily misunderstood. They could lead to the conclusion that Paul received nothing from his predecessors in the Christian faith, that he had no respect for those who were "apostles before me" (Gal. 1:17).

Such conclusions would be far from the truth. True, he did receive his gospel by revelation. But there is a difference between gospel and theology. His gospel was a realization of the saving significance of Jesus Christ. It was a proclamation of God's saving act which opened the way for all men to be saved. It was a message with a demand for a decision. All of this, Paul received by revelation at the time of his conversion. We must not limit it to mean only "his understanding of the universality of the gospel."[6] It did mean that, but it meant more. For this gospel, then, Paul claimed an independent revelation, a knowledge that came from God without human intermediaries.

But, beware! He did not mean that his gospel was different from that of the other apostles. It was the same as the gospel already believed and preached before him.[7] Fourteen (or perhaps seventeen) years after his conversion, he "laid before them [i.e., James, Peter, and John] . . . the gospel which I preach among the Gentiles" (Gal. 2:2). They accepted his gospel as being the same as theirs, and he accepted theirs as being the same as his.[8] Speaking of the other apostles, he said, "Whether then it was I or they, so we preach and so you believed" (1 Cor. 15:11). This is a claim that Paul's gospel, received by revelation, was the same gospel which the other apostles received in other ways. Writing to the Romans, a church which he did not establish and where he had not preached, he said, "I myself am satisfied about you, my brethren, that you yourselves are full of goodness, filled with all knowledge, and able to instruct one another" (Rom. 15:14). He claims that his letter was meant only as a "reminder" "on some points" (Rom. 15:16). There is no indication that Paul thought his theology was different from theirs, no indication that he was trying to correct them. Rather, he recognized their theology as essentially the same as his.

Much of what may be termed theology—the doctrines of Christ, the church, Christian living, hope, predestination, salvation history, the cross, and the work of the Holy Spirit—Paul learned from his predecessors in Christian faith and preaching. At least he learned the fundamentals of these doctrines and built upon them as foundation stones.

When did he learn it? He had many opportunities in spite of his assertion of independence in Galatians but not contrary to it.

First, many of his missionary partners were in the Christian movement from the beginning. Barnabas (Gal. 2:1), Silas (2 Cor. 1:19), Jesus Justus (Col. 4:11), and John Mark (Col. 4:10) were in the Christian movement from its earliest days. Some of them had known Jesus personally. Paul would have discussed his message with them and learned from them.

Second, he speaks of a visit to Jerusalem, three years after his conversion, when he visited Cephas for two weeks (Gal. 1:19). I am sure that they did not discuss the weather all that time. Can there be any doubt that they spoke of the life of Jesus, of the Christian message to the world, and a number of other things related to the gospel? I think not. Paul also attended Christian services while there and heard the preaching of others.

II. Paul's Use of Pre-Pauline Materials

In the past thirty years an intensely interesting and profitable field of study in New Testament has been opened up. It is a study of the most primitive Christian thought through the use of confessions and hymns that have been embodied in New Testament writers (Paul, John, Peter, and the Synoptic Gospels). A number of books [9] have been published as well as a great many articles in theological journals.[10]

It has been discovered that a number of these formulas (confessions and hymns) were included in Paul's letters (as well as other writings) and that they can be identified by certain signposts.[11] By studying those parts of his writing where he was reproducing the presuppositions from which he started, not developing his own special teaching, it is possible to reconstruct the teachings of the pre-Pauline Christian movement.[12]

What are these signposts? How can we know that a biblical passage is traditional material rather than the product of the author? The most important indications are: [13]

(1) when the author himself introduces the material as traditional by the use of such catchwords as "received," "delivered," and/or "confess";

(2) when material is included in the passage which is not in harmony with the context;

(3) when the vocabulary is different from that ordinarily used by the writer; and

(4) when the structure of the passage is clearly poetical or confessional.

To illustrate the use of these criteria, let us look at one piece of material which is almost universally recognized as being a confessional formula which Paul used to summarize his own preaching (1 Cor. 15:3-5).

Notice first that the material is introduced by the catchwords which were technical terms for receiving and passing on tradition. "For I *delivered* to you . . . what I also *received*" (v. 3). Wherever these words are found, or even one of them, one should consider the possibility that they introduce traditional material (cf. also 1 Cor. 11:23-25).

Next, notice that the material does not fit the context, at least not perfectly. Paul's concern is with the resurrection, yet the material includes statements concerning the death of Christ for our sins and his burial. These statements are not needed in this context. They are included because they were an integral part of the formula (cf. Phil. 2:6–11 for another traditional formula which does not fit the context).

Third, notice that the formula speaks of "sins" in the plural, whereas Paul usually, almost uniformly, uses "sin" only in the singular for the principle of sin. When he wants to speak of individual sins, he usually uses "transgressions" (cf. Rom. 5:16). (Cf. Rom. 1:3–4 which uses the quite un-Pauline expression, "seed of David.")

Fourth, the style of the material is definitely poetic parallelism. There are four members, each introduced by the relative pronoun "that." The four members are parallel. Notice:

> that Christ died for our sins in accordance with the scriptures,
>> that he was buried,
> that he was raised on the third day in accordance with the scriptures,
>> and that he appeared.

Paul then lists a number of the appearances of Jesus, the earliest written list we have, which probably went beyond the traditional formula and drew on his own experience (certainly v. 8 does this). (Cf. Rom 1:3–4; Col. 1:15–20 for other examples of poetic structure.)

Is this material only rarely found in Paul's epistles, or is it frequently found? As a matter of fact, it is quite frequent. Fragments of such material are found in many passages, identified by turns of phrase which are traceable to pre-Pauline times.[14] But there are also many passages which are almost complete. The following may be identified:

(1) Formulas which link the "seed of David" Christology with the resurrection (Rom. 1:2–4; 2 Tim. 2:8).

(2) Formulas which link the death and resurrection without relating the death to sin in any way (Rom. 14:9; 2 Cor. 13:4; 1 Thess. 4:14).

(3) Formulas which relate the death of Christ to sin and its forgiveness (Rom. 4:24–25; Gal. 1:4; Rom. 3:24–26; 1 Cor. 15:3–5). (Cf. also statements in which Christ is said to have died for someone—Rom. 5:6,8; 14:15; 1 Cor. 8:11; 2 Cor. 5:15; 1 Thess. 5:10; Gal. 2:21.)

(4) Formulas that focus on a title of Jesus (1 Cor. 12:3; Phil. 2:11—a formula within a formula; Rom. 10:9,10).

(5) Formulas of incarnation (Rom. 10:6,7,9; 2 Cor. 8:9; Eph. 4:10).

(6) Formulas of mediatorship (Gal. 4:5; 1 Tim. 2:5).

(7) A formula that speaks of Christ's part in creation (1 Cor. 8:5–6).

(8) A formula of his heavenly reign (Rom. 8:34).
(9) Formulas of his second advent (1 Thess. 5:2; 1 Cor. 16:22).
(10) An ecclesiastical formula (1 Cor. 11:23–26).
(11) More sophisticated formulas (1 Tim. 3:16; Phil. 2:6–11; Col. 1:15–20).

The same types of formulas can be identified in the writings of John, Hebrews, Peter, and the Synoptics. This indicates that they represent pre-Pauline formulations of the gospel.

Another source of knowledge concerning Paul's use of traditional material is found in the early chapters of Acts. C. H. Dodd has presented convincing evidence that the early chapters of Acts give a genuine report of early Christian preaching and that the letters of Paul show evidence of being based on that preaching. By comparing traditional formulas found in Paul's letters with the core messages of the sermons in the early chapters of Acts, he finds the following elements in common: [15]

(1) The age of fulfillment has dawned, the prophecies have been fulfilled, and the new age is inaugurated by Christ.

(2) This has been accomplished through the coming of Christ, who was born of the seed of David, died for our sins, and arose from the dead.

(3) The living Christ is now exalted to the right hand of God and is rightfully Lord of all men.

(4) He will come again at the consummation of the messianic age to judge the world and complete the salvation of his people.

Yet another source is available. It is Paul's first letter to the Thessalonians (2 Thess. could also probably be included here, but since this is debatable and not important to our study, we will not do so). The verdict of the scholars is that 1 Thessalonians is the least Pauline of all of Paul's letters.[16] There is no evidence of the special emphases which we have come to associate with Paul's name on the basis of Romans, Galatians, and the Corinthian letters. Since this letter is also his first, it can be accepted as a summary of the early Christian preaching which he had received.

Beare mentions several points in which the epistle shows evidence of the common faith of the Christians rather than the particular formulations of Paul.[17] Salvation is spoken of as "you turned to God from idols, to serve a living and true God" (1:9). The message they had heard was entrusted to them of God (2:4) and is called "the gospel of God" (2:8). The believers are "brethren beloved of God" (1:4) and God teaches them to love one another (4:9). The Holy Spirit is the gift of God (4:8).

From these indications and others, it is clear that Paul's proclamation had not become as Christ centered as it later did. Of course, Christ is not ignored; how could he be in preaching the gospel? But the whole tenor of the letter shows it to be a summary of the thought of early Christians "written in the style of the great apostle."[18]

From these sources, then, we can garner the main outlines of the rich theological heritage which Paul received from his predecessors.

III. Contributions of Early Christianity to Paul's Thought

How much was Paul influenced by early Christianity? This is a debated question. Some would limit it to the doctrine of Christ.[19] At least their discussion of dependence is limited to this doctrine. Others would include some elements in all his theology—"words of the Lord," the paraenetic tradition, Paul's use of the Old Testament, baptism and the Lord's Supper, the Holy Spirit, and eschatology, as well as the doctrine of Christ.[20]

The truth lies somewhere between these extremes. All agree that the main outlines of Paul's doctrine of Christ came from his predecessors. It may be accepted without too much question that the fundamental features of his doctrine of salvation, his doctrine of the church, his concept of Christian living, and his eschatology came from the same source. While his predecessors knew of and experienced the power of the Holy Spirit, it is probable that Paul's doctrine of the Holy Spirit is his own formulation. In these areas of thought we will seek to discover to what extent Paul was influenced by his Christian heritage.

1. The Doctrine of Christ

The first task of the Christian community was to come to terms with its understanding of Jesus. No doubt there is progress in this understanding, going from a very primitive and unsophisticated Christology to one that was much more sophisticated. But we will not concern ourselves primarily with this progress. Our concern is with the extent to which Paul leaned on his predecessors for his Christology.

With few exceptions, Paul's doctrine of Christ is based on the early Christian beliefs. He was not the originator of a new Christology and there was never any conflict, at this point, between him and the first believers.[21] "The decisive steps in Christology were taken before Paul's time."[22] Robert H. Nounce has argued convincingly that from the beginning "there existed a continuity of interpretation in respect to the Christ-event.[23]

(1) We begin where the early Christians began, with *the resurrection*

of Jesus of Nazareth. His disciples had known him as a rabbi and prophet, an extraordinary man of prayer, and a man whom God approved through miraculous works. When he died, they thought him dead. Their budding hopes of setting up a messianic kingdom with him at the head were crushed.

Then he arose from the dead. He appeared to them. He ascended. The Holy Spirit came in power almost at once. What did this mean? How were they to understand his gift of forgiveness and power? How were they to explain what they believed to others that others might share their blessings. This is the stuff that true theology is made of in all ages. Theology, in its true sense, is not an effort to systematize religious thought. It is an effort to explain experience and to find ways to communicate the good news of God's grace to others.

The dramatic fact of the resurrection faced them. Aside from the fact itself, the resurrection carried some important implications. One, the earthly life of Jesus had to be reassessed and fitted into God's redemptive movement. Two, the meaning of the resurrection for Jesus himself must be sought.

First, the resurrection meant that the entire event of Jesus—his ministry, teaching, and death—was a redemptive act of God. In coming to this conclusion, the disciples were only seeing with greater clarity what Jesus himself had taught when he interpreted his mission as the inauguration of the kingdom of God.[24] The resurrection meant, first of all, God's yes to man's no. Jesus had been murdered by evil men; God showed his approval by raising him from the dead (cf. Acts 1:22; 2:22–24,32; 4:10; Rom. 1:4; 8:34; 1 Thess. 4:14).

The use of the "seed of David" terminology points to their belief that in Jesus of Nazareth the promises of God had been fulfilled. Jesus was the fulfillment of prophecy, yet a fulfillment that goes beyond and supersedes the prophecy.[25]

Second, the resurrection meant the enthronement of Christ. "Let all the house of Israel therefore know assuredly that God has made him both Lord and Christ, this Jesus whom you crucified" (Acts 2:36). Perhaps the earliest Christology of all was that which looked upon the resurrection as enthronement.[26] At least, the assertion that it was contains an element of truth.

This thought is found in the ancient formula which Paul quoted as containing the content of the gospel he preached concerning the Son of God (Rom. 1:3–4).

Who was descended from David according to the flesh, and

> *designated Son of God in Power according to the Spirit of holiness by his resurrection from the dead Jesus Christ our Lord.*

The key word in the formula is "designated" (Gk. *oristhenos*). Many have called the formula a presentation of adoptionist Christology—i.e., Jesus became the Son of God at his resurrection. There can be no doubt that Jesus became something at his resurrection that he was not before it.[27] We cannot make the language mean simply that he was "proved to be" the Son of God. Both "descended" and "designated" speak of a "becoming" not of a "being."

However, to speak of this as adoptionist Christology is wrong. Notice that he was designated Son of God *with power* and *according to the Spirit of holiness.* Jesus, the human Jesus (the humanity of Jesus was not laid aside at death), had already been marked as the Son of God by the "Spirit of holiness" that dwelt within him.[28] After his resurrection, he was "installed" into a position which already belonged to him, that of "Son of God with power." The formula does not speak of a new essence, but of a new function (orthodoxy's contention that Jesus was always God's Son in essence is not threatened by the formula).

What we have then is an enthronement formula. A recitation of the faith of the early believers in terms of God's mighty act in raising Jesus from the dead and making him both Christ and Lord. It is this faith that gave the early church its reason for being and its motivation in missions.

(2) *The assertion of the saving significance of the death of Jesus* was the second plank in early Christian Christology. At first, the death of Christ was simply spoken of as having happened. No theological explanation of the cross was attempted. Three things were said with reference to it: it was according to the plan and foreknowledge of God (Acts 2:23), it fulfilled the Scriptures and was not contrary to God's promises (Acts 3:18), and it was murder (Acts 2:23; 3:15).

But it was not long before the Christian community began to ascribe redemptive significance to the cross. The resurrection made it necessary to understand the cross in such a way that it would overcome, even transform, the scandal of the curse which had been placed on Jesus (at least according to Jewish thought, cf. Gal. 3:13). The cross had to be fitted into the redemptive work of God.[29]

The earliest attempt is preserved for us in the formula preserved by Paul: "Christ died for our sins according to the scriptures" (1 Cor. 15:3, KJV). This formula probably comes from the Palestinian community;[30] if so, it would show that the death of Christ assumed redemptive mean-

THE CHRISTIAN

ing very early.

In favor of the very early linking of the death of Christ and forgiveness of sins is another formula (Rom. 3:25).[31] It reads: "Whom God put forward as an expiation by his blood, to be received by faith" (cf. Romans 4:25; Gal. 1:4; 1 Cor. 11:25).

There can be little doubt that the early Christians, long before Paul, located the decisive act of redemption in the past, not in the future.[32] The emphasis was not on the second coming[33] but "upon the victory which has already been won in the Crucifixion-Resurrection.[34] Paul took over the tradition and deepened it, but he was not the first to give the cross meaning, to see salvation in what appeared to have been a disaster.[35]

(3) *Christ as the living Lord of the church* was the third plank in early Christian Christology. The early Christians not only remembered him but celebrated his presence in their midst as the Lord of their lives and the power of their activity. "Lord" is perhaps the title that identified the living Christ with the ongoing life of the Christian movement. It was used in the early churches and became the basic title which Paul used for Jesus Christ.

The early chapters of Acts and the formulas assert that the heavenly Christ: sends his Holy Spirit on his people (Acts 2:33); adds new members to the fellowship by way of salvation (Acts 2:47); heals the sick (Acts 3:6,16); is the mediator between God and man (1 Tim. 2:5); and gives salvation to those who believe in him (Rom. 4:25), that is, who confess, "Jesus is Lord" (Rom. 10:9). Schweizer is surely right in asserting that the idea of the lordship of Christ has a continuity from the lifetime of Jesus to the Hellenistic church.[36]

(4) *Belief in the preexistence of Christ* was the fourth plank in early Christian Christology. To the modern reader, with his concern for metaphysics, it seems strange that the doctrine of preexistence (the basis of the orthodox formulation of the incarnation) played such a small role in early Christianity and practically none in the thought of Paul.

The idea of preexistence, that is, existence before his birth on earth, is found only in three Pauline passages, each of which are identifiable as pre-Pauline formulations.

The first passage reads:
Who, though he was in the form of God
did not count equality with God a thing to be grasped
but emptied himself,
taking the form of a servant,
being born in the likeness of men (Phil. 2:6–7).

There is little doubt that this hymn speaks of the preexistence of Christ, though there is one scholar, a notable exception, who argues unconvincingly that the hymn speaks only of the human existence of Jesus.[37]

The other Pauline passage which speaks of the preexistence of Christ reads:

He is the image of the invisible God,
the first-born of all creation:
for in him all things were created,
in heaven and on earth,
visible and invisible . . .
he is before all things,
and in him all things hold together (Col. 1:15–17).

That this is a pre-Pauline formula [38] or a Pauline conflation of more than one formula,[39] is indicated by the poetic structure and its strangeness in this context in Colossians (i.e., as a part of a prayer).

Many problems have arisen in Christian debate on this passage. One of which is the meaning of "the first-born of all creation." It is highly unlikely that Paul or his predecessors was thinking in terms of a *limited* preexistence for Christ. Certainly, if the phrase means nothing else, it distinguishes Christ from all other creatures, including men. It makes him unique.[40]

But it is much more likely that the phrase refers to his sovereignty over all creation. The background is the "right of primogeniture" which is common to Near Eastern cultures. The firstborn Son is the head of the household. The expression was often used to mean "prior to and supreme over." One Jewish rabbi is quoted as calling God himself the Firstborn.[41]

Plainly the passage represents a very high Christology, teaching: The preexistence of Christ, his lordship over all creatures, his function in bringing all things into existence ("principalities," etc., may be a Pauline insertion in the light of the conflict at Colossae), and his present function in making a cohesive unity in the universe.

Finally, the preexistence of Christ is hinted at in another pre-Pauline formula of six members, one of which reads: *"He was manifested in the flesh"* (1 Tim. 3:16). Preexistence is implied for Jesus. He only became manifest, not existent, at his birth.

Of course, the idea of preexistence carries with it metaphysical implication which the early church fathers laid hold of in insisting on the essential deity of Jesus, that is, his oneness of essence with the Father.

But such questions, if ever asked by New Testament writers, were never made the center of their concern.

Perhaps our modern testimony to Christ would be more effective if we returned to the biblical way of speaking of him. Metaphysical discussion of the trinity and of the essence of the divine being often obscures the essential Christian witness. Such discussion may have a place in apologetic debate; it detracts from the witness that Jesus Christ makes a real difference in the lives of those who acknowledge him as Lord of their lives.

2. The Doctrine of Salvation

Paul's most creative contribution to Christian thought is his doctrine of salvation. The great controversies of the first century forced him to explore and express the meaning of salvation more thoroughly than any other writer. Yet, he did not invent the doctrine. He began with the foundation of early Christian theology.

We note first that many of the formulas have something to say about the doctrine of salvation. The purpose of Christ's death and resurrection is said to be "that he might be Lord both of the dead and of the living" (Rom. 14:9). "Justification" is the result of his death for our "transgressions" and his resurrection (Rom. 4:25). He gave himself "for our sins to deliver us from the present evil age" (Gal. 1:4). He became poor so that we by reason of his poverty "might be rich" (2 Cor. 8:9).

In each of these formulas the basis of salvation is in the work, especially the death, of Jesus Christ. The way of receiving salvation is not expressed, but its content is expressed in various ways. "Justification," deliverance from the "present evil age," being "rich," and being under the lordship of Christ are varieties of expression. To be added to these is the formula: "This is the cup of the New Testament in my blood" (1 Cor. 11: 24–25). Here, the new covenant with its forgiveness of sins is referred back to the blood of Christ.

In the early chapters of Acts, the most persistently recurring motifs are repentance and forgiveness of sins (cf. 2:36; 3:9; 4:12; 5:30–31; 10:43). Repentance describes the radical orientation of life in God which is necessary to the reception of salvation. Forgiveness describes the content of salvation in terms of a new relationship with God, that is, acceptance into his fellowship.

Not much is said in 1 Thessalonians about salvation, but much is hinted at. The initiative comes from God who had chosen the "brethren" (1:4) and destined them (5:9) to salvation. The means by which salvation has been provided is the death of Christ (5:10). Conversion comes as a result of their response to the preaching of the gospel (1:5; 2:1–8). The content of their response was a decision, a decision to turn from idols and submit themselves as slaves to the true and living God (1:9). The results of conversion are threefold: deliverance from the wrath to come (1:10), a change in nature from men of darkness into "sons of light" (5:4–5), and life in fellowship with Christ whether dead or alive (5:9).

If these statements do not sound like the Paul you know from his great letters, they are not. He made them, but he made them before he entered into the great controversies that forced him to refine, redefine, and crystallize his doctrine of salvation. They certainly lack the richness and depth of the great apostle's later years.

On the other hand, the doctrine of salvation which our sources disclose as common to early Christian thought is not different in kind from Paul; there is only a difference of degree. The doctrine is not developed, but the main outlines are present.

3. The Doctrine of the Church

Paul did not invent the church; he found it already functioning when he was converted. As a matter of fact, he had had contact with it before his conversion; it was the "church of God" in Jerusalem which he had persecuted.

When was the church established? There can be little doubt that the roots of the church rested in the ministry of Jesus. He called a group of men around him as disciples. They were to learn his message, to become his men. He often spoke to them about the dynamics of group life and action. After his resurrection, he commissioned them to be his witnesses in all the world and promised them the Holy Spirit (Acts 1:8).

To talk about the beginning of the church is about as meaningless as to talk about the beginning of a human life. The believers began to function as a church after the resurrection; they were filled with power at Pentecost. But we know that all this was in continuity with their relationship with Jesus and his ministry to them before his death.

When we turn to the early chapters of Acts, the early formulas, and 1 Thessalonians, we learn a great many things about the church-idea which Paul found in Jerusalem and duplicated in his early ministry. Again, controversy led him to refine and define his conception of the church, but it never led him to depart from the foundational principles which he first learned in the mother church.

(1) The early church regarded itself as *a divine institution,* belonging

to God, operating under the lordship of Christ, enabled by the presence and power of the Holy Spirit.

When the church elected a successor to Judas, they sought the leadership of God and voted to follow that leadership (Acts 1:15–26. The Greek word in verse 26 which is translated "enrolled" by RSV and "numbered" by KJV really means to "vote one a place among.") [42] When faced with the ministry of witnessing, they spent ten days in prayer awaiting the coming of the Holy Spirit with power. When faced with persecution and death, they turned to God for courage to keep on witnessing and trusted him to provide for their needs (Acts 4:23–31).

When Paul wrote the Thessalonians, he addressed them as "the church . . . in God the Father and the Lord Jesus Christ" (1:1). He urged them to live a life worthy of God (2:12).

The whole record of these days show that the church understood itself as God's church. He was its reason for being, the object of its ministry; to him they belonged.

(2) The church understood itself as *a sharing partnership, a community.* The importance of this idea in their minds is undeniable. It is stated in Acts 2:42, but the meaning of the verse is obscured by the omission of an article and a comma in the English translations. It reads in them: "And they devoted themselves to the apostles' teaching and fellowship, to the breaking of bread and the prayers" (RSV). In the Greek, there is a definite article before "fellowship." The verse should read: "They devoted themselves to *the* apostle's teaching, to *the* fellowship, to *the* breaking of bread, and to *the* prayers." Thus fellowship is an equal partner with the other members of the sentence. "Fellowship" is the English word used to translate a much stronger word in the Greek *(koinonia),* a word which means partnership, sharing, and mutual involvement in each other's lives.

The importance of this concept of partnership, of community, in the early chapters of Acts is striking. Note the italicized phrases in the following verses. "All these *with one accord* devoted themselves to prayer" (1:14). "They were *all together in one place"* (2:1). "They were *all filled* with the Holy Spirit and [all] began to speak in other tongues, as the Spirit gave them [all] utterance" (2:4. Note that there was a fellowship of ministry.). "All who believed *were together* and had *all things in common"* (2:44). "And day by day, attending the temple *together* and breaking bread in their homes" (2:46). "They lifted up *their voices together* to God" (4:24). "The company of those who believed were of *one heart and one soul* " (4:32). When division threatened the unity of the church, swift action was taken to restore it (6:1–6).

First Thessalonians is quite as striking in ringing the note of community in the church. "You yourselves have been taught by God to love one another . . . But we exhort you, brethren, to do so more and more" (4:9–10). "Comfort one another with these words" (4:18). "Encourage one another and build one another up, just as you are doing" (5:11). "Be at peace among yourselves" (5:13). "Admonish the idle, encourage the fainthearted, help the weak, be patient with them all" (5:14). "See that none of you repays evil for evil, but always seek to do good to one another and to all" (5:15). "Greet all the brethren with a holy kiss" (5:26). All of these passages are full of the feeling that each member of the community should feel at one with and responsible for each other member.

(3) The church considered itself *the eschatological community*. The believers had been redeemed by the death of Christ and filled with the Holy Spirit. This was what Joel was talking about when he prophesied the signs of the end of the ages (Acts 2:1–4,16). They had been taught by Jesus that a new religion could not be contained in the old institutions of Israel. The fact that even Jewish converts must be added to the church (Acts 2:42) shows that they did not think of themselves as a part of Israel. Though their consciousness of distinction came only gradually to expression, it was there from the start.

(4) *The organization of the church* was fluid in those early days. Before the seven were elected (Acts 6:1–6), the whole life of the church seems to have been under the guidance of the twelve. However, the voice of the people had a place in the decisions of the church; the twelve were not dictators. The election of the successor to Judas was by vote of the church. Further, when need arose for the seven to administer the food program of the church, the apostles said, "Therefore, brethren, pick out from among you seven men . . . whom we may appoint to this duty" (Acts 6:3).

It was not long before other men were regularly designated as elders or bishops (the two words meant the same function). At least, the Jerusalem church had such men by the time of the relief visit of Paul and Barnabas (Acts 11:30). Paul and Barnabas also took time to lead the new churches to elect elders (Acts 14:23) as if it were normal for a church to have them.[43]

How the elders functioned is unknown. Probably, they functioned in an administrative capacity much like the elders in the Jewish synagogue. This conclusion is supported by the words of Paul: "Respect those who labor among you and are over you in the Lord and admonish you, and esteem them very highly in love because of their work" (1 Thess. 5: 12–13).

You see, the early churches were not formless, purposeless groups of people with no structure. True, they depended on the leadership of God (as all churches should); they respected those who had special gifts. They also had a structured organization and looked upon administrative ability as a gift from God quite on a par with other spiritual gifts.

Nothing is said about clerks, treasurers, and song leaders. The functions associated with these offices were no doubt performed in the first churches. If the apostles did it at first, it would not have been long before they asked for help. That statistical records were kept is shown by the statements: "there were added . . . about three thousand souls" (Acts 2:41) and "the number of the men came to about five thousand" (Acts 4:4).

(5) There seems to have been a good deal of ambivalence concerning an *appropriate name for the disciple band.* The disciples needed a name to indicate the nature of the church, that described it as unique, standing against the world and all other religions, and with God. The search for a name was probably unconscious.

In the Aramaic speaking church, the Christians may have used *kenishta* (meaning, an assembly), though this is only a guess. In the earliest period, according to Acts, no name gained an ascendency. The two most popular were "the brethren" and "the disciples." Others such as "flock" and "synagogue" were only used sparingly. Outsiders called them "the people of the way," "the sect," and "Christians."

The search ended in the adoption of a Greek term which means "an assembly" (Gk. *ekklēsia*), usually and wrongly translated in English versions by "church." The most common use of the word among the Greeks was to designate the city council of the Greek city-state. By its use in the Greek translation of the Old Testament for the *assembled congregation* of Israel, it had gained a religious connotation which it never had among the Greeks. Thus, in the Greek world, it was necessary to add "of Christ" or "of God" to distinguish the Christian church from the political churches of the day.

In settling on this name, the church rejected all names which were used for other religious groups. The Jewish "synagogue" faded quickly into the background; Greek words for religious guilds were never considered at all. The church refused to start out with the handicap of a name which placed them as one among other religious groups. Paul, in his preliterary days, may have contributed to this search for a name; it is just as likely that he found it already established among the Greek churches.

Four implications of the name chosen are possible: (1) The church is a community of people whose habit is to assemble themselves together (the word was never used for the building in which they met, though it was used for the services conducted). (2) The church was an established community not an occasional assembly; it had permanence. (3) The community had a purpose for being, and (4) the community represented something beyond itself; it was the church *of God* or *of Christ.*

(6) *The rites practiced in the church* were two—baptism and the Lord's Supper. Paul did not originate these rites, though he helped to make their meaning clear. It would seem that the theological explanation of what we call the ordinances of the church was very primitive. Paul developed the primitive conceptions, especially with regard to baptism.

The earliest record of the institution and purpose of the Lord's Supper is found in a pre-Pauline formula (1 Cor. 11:24–25). It is probable that the early Christian celebration of the Lord's Supper was associated with a common meal, a "love-feast." Paul's major condemnation of the Corinthians was that they had turned the "love-feast" into a drunken orgy (1 Cor. 11:17–22).

It was celebrated in the assembly of the church. There is no evidence that it was ever considered a private rite. Paul's instructions concerned what happened "when you assemble as a church" (1 Cor. 11:18).

It used two elements—bread and wine. Possibly the bread was used at the beginning of the love-feast and the wine at the end. The separation of the two elements could explain why, at the beginning, the two "words" are not parallel. Probably when the love-feast was eliminated and one element immediately followed the other, there came an impulse to make the "words" parallel.

The bread represented the "body" of Christ. To the Jew, this would suggest the sacrificial offering of Christ for our sins. Among the Greeks "which is broken for you" had to be added to make this meaning clear.

The cup represented, not the blood of Christ, but the new covenant established in that blood. Later, the impulse to parallelism brought this saying into harmony with the bread "word."

Always the celebration looked forward to the coming of Christ. Thus three emphases were associated with the remembrance of the Lord's Supper: the sacrificial death of Christ, the new covenant established by that death, and the promise of his coming.

The remembrance was "dynamic." Dramatic participation in the rite made these elements a part of the present and at the same time enforced the Christian's feeling of need for daily remembrance. Thus, Paul could speak of participation in the Lord's Supper as "participation in the blood of Christ" and "in the body of Christ" (1 Cor. 10:16). This is not to speak of the Lord's Supper as a magic rite which procures salvation, but as a dynamic event which involves us in the Christ event from its beginning to its end.

Baptism was certainly practiced by the early Christians (Acts 2:41). The only theological explanation of baptism in our material are the words: "be baptized . . . in the name of Jesus Christ for the forgiveness of your sins" (Acts 2:38). These words were spoken to the Jews at Pentecost and were preceded by the admonition to "repent." It is important to notice that grammatically, and therefore theologically, the phrase "for the forgiveness of sins" belongs only with "be baptized." The context makes it quite clear that baptism followed the "forgiveness of sins" which was received when one repented (Acts 3:19).

The Greek preposition *(eis)* which is translated "for" can mean with reference to. When it is associated with baptism (about fifteen times in the New Testament), it can always have that meaning and usually *must* have that meaning. Thus, the meaning of baptism is: "be baptized because your sins have been forgiven." Thus, baptism was thought to be a declaratory rite in which the new Christian took his stand in the church, and with the church for Christ. There is no room in this passage for any interpretation which would make baptism either the effective cause of or a necessary condition to the forgiveness of sins.

Thus salvation and baptism must be distinguished, though not necessarily separated in time. This does not mean that baptism was, or is, a mere physical act which only symbolizes the past event of death to sin and resurrection to a new life. Rather, it is an act (cf. Rom. 6:1-3) in which the believer is dynamically united with Christ in his death and resurrection in a public way. It reinforces the private decision of faith and involves one in the obligation to live a life that is free from the dominion of sin (Rom. 6:12-14).

Modern understanding of baptism is greatly influenced by theological debate over the centuries. It is impossible to be objective. It is impossible to avoid extremes. It is difficult to place ourselves back in the first century and see the majesty and simplicity of baptism through the eyes of the early Christians.

The following may be asserted with some confidence: (1) All who believed and were saved were expected to be baptized. (2) Only those who had believed were baptized. (3) Baptism was by immersion of the whole person in water (this is demanded both by the meaning of the Greek word and the symbolism of the act). (4) Baptism was meant to be a spiritually dynamic experience which reinforced the believer's decision and promised a new life.

Paul's references to baptism are rare. He probably adopted and carried on the interpretation of early Christians and made little change. One thing is certain. Paul did not consider baptism as a part of the gospel, a necessary condition of salvation. No one who thought of baptism in these terms could have written, as Paul did, "Christ sent me not to baptize, but to preach the gospel" (1 Cor. 1:17, KJV).[44]

4. The Nature of the Christian Life

From the start Christianity confronted its converts with the challenge to live like Christ. The Thessalonians, Paul said, "became imitators of us and of the Lord" (1:6) at their conversion. Each of Paul's letters contains a hortatory section in which he spells out in some detail what it means to live a Christian life. Paul did not formulate these details; he adopted them for his Christian predecessors. In the course of his ministry, he probably added to what he had received and gave the whole a *raison de être*. We will discuss Paul's contributions later; here we are concerned to show that Paul received a great number of his emphases on Christian behavior from his predecessors.

Even so, they were not innovators. They received much from their Jewish heritage; it was within the Jewish context that Christian living first arose. Christian Jews continued to practice their Judaism and follow the old patterns of life with the added dimension of devotion to Christ.

When the Christian mission reached the Gentile world, the problem of Christian behavior became acute. The Gentile world of the first century was extremely evil. It is said that the catalog of sins in Romans 1:18–32 is a listing of the kinds of behavior which Paul could have viewed on the streets of Corinth. New converts needed guidance, not only on the general principles of Christian living, but also on the details.

Consequently, a moral as well as a doctrinal tradition was formulated.[45] The moral tradition may have been based on a similar tradition developed by Jewish missionaries for the instruction of Gentile proselytes.[46]

A comparison of ethical instructions in Paul's letters (cf. Rom. 12–13; Gal. 5:13 to 6:10; Col. 3:5 to 4:6; Eph. 4:17 to 6:9; 1 Thess. 4:1 to 5:22) with other New Testament writers leads to the conclusion that all were indebted to such a tradition.[47] The same kind of material is found in 1 Peter and Hebrews and is preserved as well in the post-apostolic writings (cf. 1 Clement, Hermes, and the Didache).[48] Possibly this material was used to instruct candidates for baptism and could therefore be called "baptismal catechetical material."[49]

To take Colossians 3:5 to 4:6 as an example, we find that the content of the moral tradition was as follows: (1) a list of vices to be "put to death" which included both sins of the "flesh" and sins of the "spirit"; sins both disreputable and decent (?) (3:5–8); (2) a discussion of their life together in the unity of the church (3:9–17) which includes a list of virtues to be "put on" as God's chosen people; (3) a list of virtues to be developed in domestic relations between wives and husbands, children and fathers, slaves and masters (3:18 to 4:1). It is noteworthy that this section, as is common in such lists, suggests mutual obligations of one to the other, (4) an admonition to Christian prayer and service, and (5) instruction about the proper conduct of a Christian in his relations with outsiders (4:5–6).

Of course there are variations in the lists and some of what Paul says is peculiar to him; at least, parallels are not found in other writers. But it looks very much like Paul made use of a moral tradition in his instructions to his churches. Perhaps this is what he had in mind when he wrote: "I commend you because you remember me in everything and maintain the traditions even as I have delivered them to you" (1 Cor. 11:2) and "If any one is disposed to be contentious, we recognize no other practice, nor do the churches of God" (1 Cor. 11:16).

5. Eschatology—The Doctrine of Last Things

There can be little doubt that Paul held a doctrine of last things in common with his predecessors and that both drew heavily from apocalyptic Judaism for their eschatological imagery. Of course, Paul and his predecessors had one thing which the apocalyptists of Israel did not have—the experience of the living Christ who had risen from the dead. This gave them a much more sure hope and at the same time a point of reference from which to interpret the meaning of the resurrection from the dead.

(1) *The second advent of Christ, his future coming,* was a lively hope among the early Christians and with Paul. Paul describes the conversion of the Thessalonians as a turning from idols to submit as slaves to God "and to wait for his Son from heaven" (1 Thess. 1:9–10). The Greek word

which is translated, "wait," means to "await one whose coming is expected," perhaps with the added idea of patience and confidence.[50]

But the supposition of many scholars that the early Christians and Paul were completely engrossed in the second coming to the virtual exclusion of all else is false. Käsemann thinks that the history of early Christianity can be traced by "means of the original imminent expectation of the parousia, its modification and its final extinction."[51] He further adds that "the entire mission of Paul is determined by the expectation of the imminent end of the world."[52] Käsemann, in these words, expresses the opinion of a number of scholars. Even F. W. Beare thinks 1 Thessalonians is dominated by "eschatological motifs" and that this reflects "the emphasis of early preaching."[53]

The evidence is against such conclusions. First, the frequency with which the Parousia (i.e., the second advent of Christ) is spoken of in our sources—the formulas, the early chapters of Acts, and 1 Thessalonians—shows that it did not absorb the attention of the early churches or of Paul. There is no mention of the coming of Christ in any of the formulas which we have identified as pre-Pauline (with the possible exception of Phil. 2:6–11 where it may be implied; cf. also 1 Thess. 5:2; 1 Cor. 16:22). In 1 Thessalonians, the Parousia is mentioned in seven passages (1:10; 2:19; 3:13; 4:13–17; 5:1–4,8–9,23). This hardly justifies Beare's statement that the letter is "dominated" by the eschatological motifs. Third, the Parousia is mentioned in only three passages in the first eleven chapters of Acts (1:6–7; 1:11; 3:20–21). This paucity of passages which even mention the expected coming of Christ shows that it was certainly not the center of gravity in their preaching.

No, the center of gravity in the early Christian message lay in the past, in Christ's first coming, in the victory already won on Calvary, with no attempt to "pry into the mystery of the future."[54] Further, the method of Paul's missionary working shows that he did not think of himself as "a delirious reporter of the near end." He did not rush around proclaiming that the world was about to end; rather, he took time to proclaim the gospel, organize churches for the continued extension of the gospel, and to train fellow workers in what Conzelmann thinks was "a Pauline school."[55]

This does not mean that Paul did not *hope* Christ would return during his own lifetime. Both in 1 Thessalonians 4:17 and 1 Corinthians 15:51, he places himself among those who will be alive at the Parousia by the use of the personal pronoun "we." But he never categorically states that Christ will come before his own death, and he seems to contemplate the possibility of his own death in Philippians 1:21 and 2 Corinthians 1:8. With Paul, as with his fellow Christians, the coming of Christ does not belong to the "faith" but to the "hope." [56]

Nor need we think that the expectation, the hope, of Christ's coming faded and disappeared. As we have shown, the so-called "imminent expectation" of the end of the world is a figment of the imagination of modern scholars rather than a conclusion drawn from New Testament evidence. It did not "disappear" from the New Testament because it never "appeared." It would be well for it to "disappear" from modern discussion. True, Paul did not mention the Parousia in Ephesians or Colossians, nor did he in Galatians. His discussion of it was dictated by the needs of his audiences. If it was important to them, he discussed it. If not, he treated it as a presupposition.

Nor was the thought of Christ's coming wrapped up in apocalyptic symbols so as to hide its real nature. Two passages in Paul make use of such symbols (1 Thess. 4:16; 1 Cor. 15:52), but the prominent thing in his thought of the second coming was with the consummation of salvation.

Paul, like Jesus before him, warned of the unexpectedness of the Parousia (1 Thess. 5:1–4) and refused to have anything to do with setting up schedules for the event.[57] In the only two passages where any kind of schedule is mentioned (1 Thess. 4:13–17; 1 Cor. 15:23–28), no mention is made of the wicked dead, the end of the world, or any of the other events which some men have worked into a "program" for the second coming.

(2) Paul believed, along with his fellow Christians, in the *future resurrection of the body*. For him, this was absolutely essential to a full and blissful life. He recoiled from the Greek idea of being "found naked" (2 Cor. 5:3), that is, divested of any body at all. He mentions by implication his thought about the Christian who dies before the coming of Christ. He thinks of them as "asleep," but this hardly means unconscious because "God will bring with him those who have fallen asleep" (1 Thess. 4:14). His concern in this passage is with the fear that these departed Christians will miss out on the second coming and resurrection. He speaks with longing of dying as "gain" and of departing to "be with Christ" as "far better" than earthly life (Phil. 1:21–23). We can conclude from these hints that the Christian who has died is with God, is better off than he was on earth, and that his bliss will not be complete before the resurrection. Beyond that, it is impossible to go on the basis of Paul's letters or the early Christian formulas.

When will the dead rise? Many scholars have found a contradiction in Paul. They point to 1 Thessalonians 4:13–18 and 1 Corinthians 15:23–28 as plainly stating that the resurrection will take place at the second coming of Christ. They point to Philippians 1:21–23 as implying that it will take place at the death of the Christian (cf. also 2 Cor. 5:1–5). They point to Colossians 3:1 and Ephesians 2:4–7 as meaning that Paul had renounced the idea of a "physical" resurrection in the future for the idea of "spiritual" resurrection in the present.[58] It seems to me that all such efforts are misplaced. They try to force the language of Paul into molds that would have been strange to him. His plain statements should rule our interpretation. If so, the time of the resurrection is at the second advent. Whether or not there is a "preliminary" clothing of the Christian before then must be a subject of speculation.

The main point, however, is to insist that Paul thought of *resurrection* not *resuscitation*. He did not look on resurrection, as the Jews who believed in the resurrection seemed to have, as simply a return to the old body. Resurrection was a lifting of the whole personality of man to a new level of existence, and this meant that the resurrection body was not only "new" but "different in kind." The present body is an "earthly tent"; the future body will be "a building from God, a house not made with hands, eternal in the heavens" (2 Cor. 5:1). It will be a "spiritual body" (perhaps, meaning adapted to spiritual existence), "imperishable," "glorious," "powerful," "in the image of Christ," "immortal" (1 Cor. 15:42–53), a body which swallows up "death" in "victory" (1 Cor. 15:54–55). It will have continuity with our present life like the plant has continuity with the seed (1 Cor. 37–38). It will be transformation of our present body into the likeness of "his glorious body" (Phil. 3:23). Won't that be something!

In other words, the resurrection and the life that follows will be the consummation of salvation for the righteous, that is, those who have been saved by the grace of God. "Salvation is nearer to us now than when we first believed" (Rom. 13:11), that is, the consummation of salvation. Paul does not describe heaven. He thinks of it as being "glorified with him" with a glory the anticipation of which makes present sufferings insignificant (Rom. 8:17–18). It will be the full harvest of which the possession of the Holy Spirit is but "the first fruits" (Rom. 8:23). It will be accompanied by the transformation of creation to share the "glorious liberty" of the sons of God (Rom. 8:20–21). It will herald the passing away of imperfect knowledge which will be replaced by perfect knowledge (1 Cor. 13:9). it will introduce "face to face" sight to replace the dark vision of God which we now have (1 Cor. 13:12). It will be a life in which "faith, hope, and love" abide forever (1 Cor. 13:13).

(3) Paul has little to say about *the unrighteous man's future*. He certainly believed in the judgment of all men and transferred the Old Testament conception of the "day of the Lord" to Christ (Rom. 2:5; 1 Cor. 1:8). The fate of the unrighteous following judgment is not emphasized, but is mentioned. It will be "sudden destruction" (1 Thess. 5:3), an experience of the "wrath of God" (1 Thess. 5:9; Rom. 2:5) which will consist of "tribulation and distress for every human being who does evil" (Rom. 2:9). One thing is certain; Paul was no universalist. He expected some to be finally lost because they had not submitted themselves to God in Christ.

(4) Paul did not use his hope for the future to satisfy the curiosity of men, but *to encourage believers to steadfast Christian living*. Hope cast its glory before it and made the Christian pathway a bright one. It was to be used to "comfort one another" (1 Thess. 4:18), to encourage the increase of brotherly love (1 Thess. 1:12), to live soberly, "put on the breastplate of faith and love, and . . . a helmet of the hope of salvation" (1 Thess. 5:8). Christian hope made present sufferings bearable (Rom. 8:17–18). It supported the exhortation: "Let us then cast off the works of darkness and put on the armor of light; let us conduct ourselves becomingly as in the day, not in reveling and drunkenness, not in debauchery and licentiousness, not in quarreling and jealousy. But put on the Lord Jesus Christ, and make no provision for the flesh, to gratify its desires" (Rom. 13:12–14). Finally, Christian hope assures that our "labor in the Lord" would not be empty of results and encourages us to be "steadfast, immovable, always abounding in the work of the Lord" (1 Cor. 15:58).

NOTES

1. Ernst Käsemann, *New Testament Questions* (Philadelphia: Fortress Press, 1969) p. 249.
2. A. M. Hunter, *Paul and His Predecessors* (Philadelphia: Westminster Press, c. 1961), p. 9.
3. Bornkamm, *Paul,* p. 113.
4. Philippe H. Menoud, "Revelation and Tradition," *Interpretation,* April, 1953, p. 137.
5. Bornkamm, *op. cit.,* p. 113.
6. Tasker, *The Old Testament in the New Testament,* p. 81.
7. Menoud, *op. cit.* p. 134.   8. James Stewart, *A Man in Christ,* p. 204.
9. Hunter, *op. cit.;* Vernon H. Neufeld, *The First Christian Confessions* (Grand Rapids: Wm. B. Eerdmans, 1963); R. H. Fuller, *Foundations of New Testament Christology* (New York: Charles Scribner's Sons, 1965); Ferdinand Hahn, *The Titles of Jesus in Christology* (New York: The World Publishing Company, 1969).

10. Menoud, *op. cit.* Others will be cited in this chapter.
11. Bornkamm, *Paul*, p. 112.
12. G. Ernest Wright and R. H. Fuller, *The Book of the Acts of God*, p. 302.
13. Ethelbert Stauffer, *New Testament Theology* (London: SCM Press, 1955), pp. 338–9, cf. Eduard Schweizer, *Lectures at the University of Zürich*, 1963.
14. Werner Kramer, *Christos, Kurios, Gottessohn* (Zürich: Zwingli Verlag, 1963), pp. 15–59.
15. *The Apostolic Preaching and Its Developments* (New York: Harper and Row, 1964), pp. 17–24.
16. Johannes Munck, "1 Thessalonians 1:1–10 and the missionary preaching of Paul," *New Testament Studies*, 9, pp. 95–110; Edward Blair, "The First Epistle to the Thessalonians," *Interpretation*, April, 1948, pp. 208–17; F. W. Beare, "Thessalonians, First," IDB 4:621–25.
17. Beare, *Ibid.*, p. 625.   18. *Ibid.*, p. 625.
19. Fuller, *Foundations*, Hahn, *op. cit.*, Kramer, *op. cit.*   20. Hunter, *Predecessors*.
21. Elias Andrews, *The Meaning of Christ for Paul*, p. 20.
22. Hunter, *Predecessors*, p. 79.
23. "Continuity of the Primitive Tradition," *Interpretation*, October, 1959, pp. 417–424.
24. Wright and Fuller, *Acts of God*, p. 289.   25. Schweizer, *Lectures, op. cit.*
26. John H. Hayes, "The Resurrection as Enthronement and the Earliest Church Christology," *Interpretation*, July, 1968, pp. 333–45.
27. Ernst Käsemann, *An Die Römer* (Tübingen: J. C. B. Mohr, 1973), p. 9.
28. W. C. Van Unnik, "Jesus the Christ," *New Testament Studies* 8, pp. 101–16.
29. Bultmann, *Theology*, Vol. 1, pp. 45–46.
30. Hans Conzelmann ("On the Analysis of the Confessional Formula in 1 Corinthians 15:3–5, *Interpretation*, Jan., 1966, p. 15) feels that the evidence is not conclusive on this point.
31. Bultmann, *op. cit.* p. 46.   32. Wright and Fuller, *Acts of God*, pp. 292–3, 307.
33. Käsemann, *Perspectives on Paul*, p. 45.
34. Bernhard Anderson, *Rediscovering the Bible* (New York; Association Press, 1951), p. 261.
35. Käsemann, *Perspectives*, p. 45.
36. Eduard Schweizer, "Discipleship and Belief in Jesus as Lord from Jesus to the Hellenistic Church," *New Testament Studies*, Nov. 1955, p. 98.
37. Charles H. Talbert, "The Problem of Pre-existence in Philippians 2:6–11," *Journal of Biblical Literature*, June, 1967, pp. 141–153.
38. Otto A. Piper, "The Saviour's Eternal Work," *Interpretation*, July, 1949, pp. 286–298. cf. Ernst Käsemann, "Eine urchristliche Taufliturgie," *Festschrift Rudolf Bultmann Aum 65. Geburtstag* (Uberreicht, 1949), pp. 133–48.
39. James M. Robinson ("A Formal Analysis of Colossians 1:15–20," *Journal of Biblical Literature*, Dec., 1957, pp. 286–298) argues that the hymn consists of two units which have been partly conflated and supplemented. He agrees: "There is compelling reason to assume the incorporation of a pre-Pauline liturgical unit in Colossians" (p. 287).
40. Piper, *op. cit.*, p. 293. Cf. Eduard Lohse, *Colossians and Philemon* (Philadelphia: Fortress Press, c. 1971), p. 48.
41. C. F. D. Moule, *The Epistles to the Colossians and to Philemon* (Cambridge University Press, 1957), p. 65. cf. Lohse, *op. cit.*, p. 49.
42. G. Abbott-Smith, *A Manual Greek Lexicon of the New Testament* (Edinburgh: T. & T. Clark, 1950).
43. Wright and Fuller, *Acts of God*, p. 313.   44. Hunter, *Predecessors*, p. 65.
45. *Ibid.*, p. 52.   46. *Ibid.*, p. 54.
47. *Ibid.*, p. 53.   48. *Ibid.*, p. 53.
49. Davies, *Paul and Rabbinic Judaism*, p. 129.   50. Abbot-Smith, *op. cit.*, p. 31.
51. Käsemann, *New Testament Questions*, pp. 236–7.   52. *Ibid.*, p. 241.
53. "Thessalonians, First," IDB. V. 3, p. 624.
54. B. W. Anderson, *Rediscovering the Bible*, p. 261.
55. Hans Conzelmann, "Paulus und die Weisheit," *New Testament Studies*, 12, p. 233.
56. Hans Conzelmann, "On the Analysis of the Confessional Formula in 1 Corinthians 15:3–5," *Interpretation*, Jan. 1966, p. 23.
57. We will discuss all Pauline material on this subject in this connection even though it may not have been derived from his predecessors.
58. Buck and Taylor, *Saint Paul*, p. 117.

PART II
Paul: Adversary of the Judaizers

4
THE COURSE OF THE CONFLICT

"Dogs," "deceitful workmen," "boastful," "troublemakers," "perverters of the gospel," "false brethren," "spies," "evil-workers," "presumptuous," and "enemies of the cross of Christ." Strange language from the apostle of Jesus Christ, isn't it? But no invective was too severe, Paul thought, for those who threatened to pervert the gospel, destroy his converts, and fragment the Christian movement. Who were these men whose "strongholds" Paul set himself to tear down? We call them Judaizers, that is, men who sought to erase the lines between Christianity and Judaism. The war cry of the Judaizers was, "Salvation is for the Jews only." They are God's chosen people. To be saved, Gentiles must not only believe in Jesus Christ; they must also be circumcized and become adopted Jews. In spite of Paul's invective, they were probably sincere Christians who were "Torah-enthusiasts." [1] Paul's invective may point more to the results of the movement than to the motivation of his opponents.

Paul was right! The movement, if successful, would have changed not only the gospel but the history of the world. The Jerusalem church would have turned into a "sect of Judaism" and the Gentile Christianity would have dissolved "into a welter of non-historical mystery cults." [2] No phase of New Testament history is more important to modern Christian thought than Paul's conflict with the Judaizers. In it, and through it, our greatest epistles were written. Think of our poverty if we did not have Galatians and Romans. If the writing of Galatians was "an epochal event in the history of religious thought," [3] what could be said about writing of Romans? In Romans as well as Galatians, "Paul has raised some of the most fundamental and far-reaching questions which can be raised in the field of religion." [4]

I. The Battle Lines Drawn

Nothing much is known about these heretics (Judaizers is our name for them, not Paul's) except from Paul's epistles and Acts 15. The course of the conflict is anything but clear and must be tentatively reconstructed by careful analysis of our sources.

1. *Roots of the Conflict*

The roots of the conflict lay in the Jewishness of Christianity at the first. Before the martyrdom of Stephen, the Christian movement was centered in Jerusalem and was a mission to the Jews only. Only Jews were saved; they kept the Jewish law and worshiped in the Jewish Temple. Circumcision was not an issue for all were circumcised.

To the Jerusalem church, this seemed proper. Had not Jesus himself said, "Salvation is of the Jews" (John 4:22, KJV)? Not understanding the implications of Jesus' commission to them, they expected all who were saved to be Jews. In those early months (or years?), the Pharisees, the arch-promoters of the Torah did not bestir themselves against the Christians. The opposition arose from the Saduccees and focused on the question of the resurrection rather than the law. The relation between Christianity and the Mosaic law was not clearly answered; indeed, it was not "clearly asked." [5] Perhaps they expected a number of Gentiles to be incorporated into their movement, a number sufficient to fill up the "full quota of the elect," left short by the unbelief of so many Jews. If so, they must have thought of them as coming to Christ through Israel, by incorporation as proselytes.[6]

According to Acts, the ministry of the Jerusalem church was confined to Jews, both natural and proselyte. Peter's mission to Cornelius' house was not a real exception. Cornelius was a devout man, that is, semi-adherent of the Jewish religion. The church could and did rejoice that God had granted repentance unto life to such "Gentiles" (Acts 11:18). Still, the Jewish believers were not willing to accept Cornelius and his kind as equal in all things. Peter must answer to the church, not so much for preaching to them, but for eating with them. The question was: "Why did you go to uncircumcised men and eat with them?" (Acts 11:3).

Even when the church was scattered abroad, following the martyrdom of Stephen, it is said: "They were all scattered throughout the region of Judea and Samaria, *except the apostles*" (Acts 8:1, italics mine). Why should they leave? The Jewish persecutors, led now by Pharisees, had no quarrel with them. They had not spoken, as Stephen had, against the Temple and the law.

Thus, the early Jerusalem church saw no difficulty in the law. All were circumcised; all kept the law. Stephen and his friends terrified them.

"Good riddance," they probably said when they were forced to flee. But the canker, though hidden, was already eating at the vitals of Christianity. The attitude of the Jerusalem church, at this time, was exactly that of the Judaizers later. "Salvation was of the Jews," therefore it must be *for* Jews. The church was the "true Israel," the community of the last times. Since the question did not arise, they saw no inconsistency between keeping the law and having faith in Christ and thinking that their salvation depended on both alike.[7]

There were exceptions. Stephen and his friends did not go along with common opinion. More clearly than others, though not clearly, they saw the logical implications of faith in Christ: it forced the rejection of the law and the Temple services as ways of coming to God. Stephen was a debater who got killed for debating. When the men of the Jewish synagogue could not stop him with words, they stopped him with stones. The accusation at his trial was: "This man never ceases to speak words against this holy place and the law" (Acts 6:13). Stephen was a Greek-Jew, a Jew of the dispersion. He and his fellows were probably not as zealous for the law as the Jerusalem Jews. Stephen, at least, saw that the law and the gospel could not coexist in any religious system. His stand made the decisive step; he is rightly called the founder of the "world mission party," a movement into which Paul was integrated from the beginning of his ministry in Antioch. But still, the question of the relation of Christianity to the law had neither been clearly asked nor answered.

2. Occasion for the Conflict

The occasion for the conflict was the spread of the gospel to the Gentiles and to Gentile lands. This began at Antioch. The record states: "Now those who were scattered because of the persecution . . . traveled as far as Phoenicia and Cyprus and Antioch, *speaking the word to none except Jews.* But there were some of them, men of Cyprus and Cyrene, who on coming to Antioch *spoke to the Greeks also,* preaching the Lord Jesus" (Acts 11:19–20, italics mine). The Jerusalem church heard of the movement (Did they know Greeks had been received?) and sent Barnabas to investigate. He approved, *correctly assessing the stand of the apostles and the majority in Jerusalem,* brought Paul to Antioch, and entered with him into the ministry of the church (Acts 11:22–26). Later, under the sponsorship of that church, he and Paul made their first momentous visit to the region of Galatia and founded the first Gentile churches (Acts 13–14).

THE COURSE OF THE CONFLICT 69

This was too much! Some "zealots for the law" in the Jerusalem church watched aghast. The question had finally been asked. What was the relation of Christianity to the Mosaic law and institutions? They knew the answer. They must save the church from ruin. They rushed to Antioch and began to teach: "Unless you are circumcised according to the custom of Moses, you cannot be saved" (Acts 15:1). This reconstruction of events conforms to general opinion among New Testament scholars.[8] It is probably correct. Buck and Taylor object; they feel that the whole problem arose first in Galatia, lasted one short, fiery year, and was settled at the Jerusalem conference (Acts 15).[9] However, they base their rather eccentric chronology of Paul's life on their supposed ability to trace Paul's life through his developing thought as revealed by his letters, an undertaking which has been termed "a failure" by the majority of New Testament scholarship.[10]

3. Orthodox Solution to the Question

The orthodox solution to the question came at the Jerusalem conference (Acts 15; Gal. 2:1–10). The two passages seem to be two reports of the same conference, though many have denied this, and no one has been able to reconcile Paul's statements about his relations to Jerusalem (Gal. 1:14 to 2:10) with the accounts in Acts. Paul makes the conference visit the second visit to Jerusalem following his conversion. The second visit, according to Acts, is the occasion when Paul and Barnabas brought relief to Jerusalem from the church at Antioch (Acts 11:27–30). The conference visit would then, according to Acts be the third visit (or even the fourth if the true reading in Acts 12:25 is "Barnabas and Saul returned *to* Jerusalem" rather than "*from* Jerusalem" as our English translations have it).

Various solutions have been offered. Some suppose that Luke has been confused by his sources and included two accounts of the relief visit (Acts 21:15–17) as if they were two visits. Others have suggested that none of the apostles was present at the famine visit (Acts 11:27–30), and thus Paul saw no need to mention it in claiming independence of those who were apostles before him. Others have solved it by equating the famine visit (Acts 11:27–30) with a private conference which Paul records in Galatians. They make the conference of Acts 15 an entirely different occasion.

None of these possible solutions is satisfactory. To suppose that a private conference between Paul and the "pillar apostles" took place at the time of the famine visit of which the church in Jerusalem knew nothing does not explain the rise of trouble in Galatia which must later be settled by a full church council. To suppose that Luke was confused in his chronology is repugnant, even though chronology was not his purpose in writing. To suppose that Paul failed to mention one or two visits to Jerusalem because they seemed unimportant to him and irrelevant to the issue is unrealistic. Why should he open himself up so needlessly to criticism?

If we ignore the chronological problem, the course of the conflict seems clear. It came to a head in Antioch, not having been viewed as a problem by Paul before that. First Thessalonians shows no knowledge of the problem. Circumcision would not be a problem except when it was preached as a theological necessity.

When Paul and Barnabas returned from their first missionary journey, they had "no small dissension and debate" with the preachers of circumcision (Acts 15:2). Following a "revelation" of God's Spirit (Gal. 2:2), they decided to take the matter to Jerusalem to be considered by the "apostles and elders" (Acts 15:2). Others were appointed to go by the church in Antioch (Acts 15:2). As a part of the delegation, or by the personal choice of Paul, Titus, a notable Gentile Christian, was taken along (Gal. 2:1). The matter was considered at length and with "much debate" (Acts 15:7). From here on the account in Acts and the account by Paul varies. Paul tells of private conferences; Acts of public decisions. Those familiar with the workings of religious conferences will understand that a decision could only be arrived at by both.

Privately, Paul laid the whole matter before those who were of "repute" in the church (Gal. 2:2), among whom were James, Cephas, and John (v. 9), the "pillar" apostles. For some reason, Titus was made a test case and some (whether the pillar apostles or the false brethren is unclear) wished to compel his circumcision (v. 3). From whatever source the demand came, it did not carry the day. Some brethren (Paul calls them "false brethren") made their way into the private conference and attacked Paul. He saw their action as an attempt to destroy the "freedom" from the law which his Gentile converts had which he himself practiced at times, and he refused to give ground for a moment (v. 5). The outcome was that the pillar apostles recognized the validity of Paul's gospel and the correctness of his action among the Gentiles. Like Barnabas, when the question became clear, the answer was apparent to them. They denied that the troublemakers had their sanction.[11] They extended (formally and in public perhaps) the right hand of Christian fellowship, recognized the divine source of Paul's commission to evangelize the Gentiles, and only asked that he "remember the poor" (vv. 7–10).

Private acceptance was followed by public vindication. When the debate was over, Peter reminded them of his experience at the house of Cornelius. He insisted that God made no "distinction between us [Jewish Christians] and them, but cleansed their hearts by faith" (Acts 15:7–9). He then pointed out the incongruity of putting a yoke around the Gentiles' necks which the Jews had not been able to bear (vv. 10–11).

James then reminded the congregation of the experience of Peter and showed that the entrance of the Gentiles into salvation fulfilled the prophecies of Israel's prophets of events in the "last days" (vv. 13–18). He then pronounced the decision publicly (Was it voted by the church?). Paul and his side were completely vindicated. Gentile converts would not need to be circumcised to be saved. The unity of the church was preserved. The gospel which saves was saved. Gentile converts were asked to observe certain restrictions on their freedom for the sake of their Jewish neighbors. But these restrictions were not necessary to salvation; they were looked upon as concessions to the scruples of weaker brethren (vv. 19–21).

Then began the victory march. The decision was embodied in a letter, and official delegates from Jerusalem accompanied Paul and Barnabas to Antioch where the letter was read and the victory celebrated.

Victory? Yes and no! The official and orthodox gospel of the churches had been formulated on this matter. But the Judaizers were unconvinced. They still must save the church, the gospel, and the cause of God. They determined to follow the steps of Paul and settle this matter at the "grassroots" of the Christian movement. The trail grows dim again. Probably, Paul (now with Silas as his companion) went back and visited the churches of Galatia and then under the leadership of the Holy Spirit made the decisive geographical step to Greece with the gospel. After two years of preaching, he returned again to Jerusalem and then to Antioch to rest before resuming his missionary travels.

Did Timothy go back overland to visit his home? Possibly. He learned that the Judaizers had been at work in the churches and driven them to the brink of apostasy. Paul, with burning spirit, composed the letter to the Galatians and sent it to the churches.

The battle was on! Where did it lead? When did it end? Philippians 3 deals with the problem. There must have been an outbreak there. Romans deals with the broad principles raised by the conflict with a sobriety that indicates that the conflict was over. If so, the conflict was not long, possibly lasting from five to ten years. There is no evidence of it in the post-apostolic churches.[12] Victory was won! The pure gospel of Jesus Christ was preserved for us. The great questions had been asked and answered, not only for that day but for our day as well.

II. The Vital Issues at Stake

Many issues were at stake in this controversy. If the gospel of Paul had not won out, Christianity would have become a mere appendage to the Jewish faith. It would never have had the influence and power in the world that it has had over the past twenty centuries. The exact issues are not present in our world, but the same kind of issues are, and have arisen time after time in Christian history.

1. The Way of Salvation

Essentially the conflict was between rival ways of salvation. The questions which arose may be stated as follows:

(1) What is wrong with man? The Judaizers divided men into two groups—Jews and Gentiles. Jews were fundamentally righteous; they needed only to keep the law of Moses to win acceptance with God. Gentiles were totally sinful. If they wanted to share in Israel's salvation, they must have faith in Christ. But they must be incorporated into the Jewish nation, be circumcised, and obey the law of Moses as well. Paul insisted that all men were lost; the trouble with man lay in a deep-seated rejection of God and rebellion against his authority. Jew and Gentile alike must be forgiven of past sins; they must be made over into the image of the living Christ.

(2) What is God's role in salvation? To the Judaizer, God was the righteous judge. He demanded perfect obedience to his will; he would accept only that man who rendered such obedience. While Paul admitted that perfect obedience from the cradle to the grave would bring life, he insisted that the sinfulness of men rendered such obedience impossible. For all practical purposes the law was not a way of salvation. Salvation came only through the gracious initiative of a holy God, who moved in love to bring men to acceptance with himself. Grace and works were contrasted as irreconcilable opposites.

(3) What part does the cross of Christ play in salvation? It is not clear what role the Judaizers gave to the cross. They were Christian, at least to the extent of believing that Christ was the promised Messiah of Israel, but it is not clear how they viewed the cross. Paul said their doctrine made the cross meaningless (Gal. 2:21). There is no doubt about the way that Paul viewed it. He ascribed to the cross of Christ a determinative

role in salvation. He saw the cross as the way in which the grace of God opened the way for the salvation of sinful men. He saw the sufferings of Christ as vicarious, that is, in our behalf.

(4) How is salvation to be received? The answer of the Judaizers was clear; salvation comes through the keeping of the law *and* faith in Christ. The answer of Paul is equally clear; salvation comes through faith alone.

(5) What is the nature of salvation? The Judaizers described salvation in terms of acceptance with God—that is, justification. But this justification came only when man had earned it. Paul saw justification as a vital and life-changing experience of the grace of God. God, paradoxically, justified, that is, received as righteous, those who were sinners. He did this by grace through faith. The act of God was no mere forensic fiction, as many scholars have insisted; it was a dynamic act of forgiveness in which righteousness was implanted in the heart of man.

(6) When does salvation occur? To the Judaizers, salvation was a hope for the future, a goal to be attained at the end. To Paul, salvation was an experience of the present, the assurance of the future, a foretaste of heaven.

2. The Role of Israel

To the Judaizers, salvation was of the Jews and for the Jews. Israel must continue to play its vital role as the servant of God. Only within the nation could salvation come. The promises of God to Israel could not be bypassed. To Paul also, salvation was of the Jews, but not for the Jews only. It was for all men. God's promises were irrevocable, but they did not attach themselves to the fleshly Israel. Indeed fleshly Israel had played its role in spite of its sins, but its unbelief had removed it from the role of the servant of God. The true descendants of Abraham were men of faith in all races. Believers were the new Israel. National Israel could be saved, and would be saved, but only by being regrafted individually into the tree of life through faith.

3. The Purpose of the Mosaic Law

To the Judaizers, the Mosaic law was God's final word. All things were to be judged by it. To Paul, the Mosaic law was a temporary expedient to force men to come to Christ. Coming after the promises to Abraham, the law could not invalidate the promise but only serve in the interests of the promises. The coming of Christ, the true content of the promise to Abraham, had invalidated the law. It could serve neither to bring men to salvation nor to guide their Christian life.

4. The Nature of the Christian Life

To the Judaizers, the Christian life consisted of keeping the law and its commandments. To Paul, the Christian life was a life of freedom under the guidance and power of the Holy Spirit. To him, as to the Judaizers, it must be a life of righteousness; sin must be avoided and overcome. But it was more than that. The Christian must live a life of responsible freedom in the church and in society as a whole. He must, with the help of the Holy Spirit, develop in Christlikeness—this was his goal.

NOTES

1. Bultmann, *Theology*, p. 108. 2. Bornkamm, *Paul*, p. 42.
3. Ernest DeWitt Burton, *A Critical and Exegetical Commentary on the Epistle to the Galatians* (Edinburgh: T. & T. Clark, c. 1921), p. lxv.
4. *Ibid.*, p. lxiv. 5. Bultmann, *op. cit.*, p. 54.
6. F. F. Bruce, *The Defence of the Gospel in the New Testament* (Grand Rapids: Wm. B. Eerdmans, 1959), p. 70.
7. Bultmann, *op. cit.*, pp. 54–55.
8. Cf. *ibid.*, p. 108; Bornkamm, *op. cit.*, p. 32.
9. *Saint Paul*, p. 249.
10. W. G. Kümmel, "Das Problem der Entwicklung in der Theologie des Paulus," *New Testament Studies*, 19 (July '72), pp. 457–458. This is a report of a consensus of the Pauline Seminar at the meeting of an international New Testament Society in 1971.
11. Buck and Taylor, *op. cit.*, p. 253.
12. Bornkamm, *op. cit.*, p. 34.

5
DEAD IN SIN

"Ungodly, wicked, senseless, fools, haters of God, haughty, faithless, heartless, ruthless, under the power of sin, sinners, enemies of God, slaves of sin, devoid of righteousness, living in the flesh, captives, wretched, weak, ineffectual, hostile to God, unable to please God, corrupt, afraid"—these are the terms in which Paul speaks of the plight of man without Christ. Even this list is not exhaustive; it is restricted to words in Romans and not even all of them. But these are enough to show that Paul looked upon man without Christ as in need of redemption.

Paul's first answer to the Judaizers is that all men, both Jews and Gentiles, are sinners and dead in sin. Not only must the Gentiles be forgiven; Jews also needed salvation! In saying this, Paul stood against the Judaizers and stands against popular opinion today.

The Judaizers thought that the Jew, because he belonged to Israel and was circumcised was already in fellowship with God. He must obey the law and do God's will. This was his task, but he was already in the *sphere* of salvation and needed only to live like it.

A popular opinion in our world today is that all men are basically good, that sin consists only of moral lapses caused by demonic influences. Man, left to himself, is good. Society is evil, they say, and at fault for the wrongs of individual men. The alcoholic is diseased; the criminal is driven by society to crime; the establishment man is compelled by society to be engrossed in this world. No one is held accountable for his own life, for his life is not determined by his own choice.

Against these extremes, Paul stood firm in his convictions that man was a sinner, that his sin came from his own choice, that he was accountable to God, and that if left to himself, he would destroy himself. Man's only hope lay in God. Salvation was a universal necessity. For it is with reference to the gospel that Paul speaks of man and his sin. He does not enter into a philosophical discussion of man's nature or origins. He deals with man in his historical context as the object of God's love and grace.[1]

Sin is never discussed for its own sake, but for the sake of the gospel. The gospel rules his thought; and just because it does, sin must be discussed.

I. Romans 1:18 to 3:20

Paul's primary discussion of sin is found in this passage. The keynote of the passage is the words: "accountable to God" (3:19). God's condemnation of man is right and just and good. The Judaizers' contention is repudiated in the words: "For no human being will be justified in his sight by works of the law since through the law comes knowledge of sin" (3:20).

The passage begins with the statement: "The wrath of God is revealed from heaven" (1:18). Paul has no problem in speaking of the "wrath of God." He believed it was real and that it is as much an expression of his character as redemption is. Paul's usual word for wrath *(orgē)* speaks of a settled disposition of opposition to evil. The common word for an outburst of temper *(thumos)* is seldom used when speaking of God's wrath; in Paul, it is found only in Romans 2:8, but then in conjunction with *orgē*.[2]

Both words are parabolic. God's wrath is not thought of as an emotion, but as an event, that is, the visitation of judgment. The "day of wrath" is the day when "God's righteous judgment will be revealed" (Rom. 2:5). Paul wanted to say that the "curse of sin" was not an impersonal nemesis or the result of cause-effect relationship.[3] Three times in chapter 1, Paul says that "God gave them up" (vv. 24,26,28). He thought that behind the so-called "natural" results of sin, God is working, though his hand be hidden.

God's wrath, Paul says, is impartial (2:11). "He will render to every man according to his works" (2:6). This means "tribulation and distress for every human being who does evil, the Jew first and also the Greek" (2:9).

Why do men stand under the wrath of God? The case of the Gentile is discussed first (1:18–32). The trouble is not that the Gentile does not know God; he does, or, at least, he can. The created world reveals God to those who look for him in it (1:19–20). This leaves the Gentile "without excuse" for his sin (1:20). His trouble is that, by choice, the Gentile "did not honor him as God or give thanks to him" (1:21). This was his rebellion; he refused to admit the truth and tried to suppress it (1:18).

The result of the Gentiles' rebellion is a "sinister perversion of life."[4] The creature takes the place of the Creator. He becomes a "fool" and creates a religion of and for himself (1:22–23). In Paul's day this took the form of gross idolatry; in our day it takes different forms. But man's rebellion against God is marked by his own self-exaltation. He becomes the center of his own world; this is his "religion." [5]

In judgment on his rebellion, God gives him up "to impurity" (1:24), "to dishonorable passions" (1:26), and "to a base mind and to improper conduct" (1:28). The sins by which man corrupts and destroys himself are a revelation of God's wrath. The catalog of these "cursed" sins runs the whole gamut of human behavior. It includes disreputable sins like sexual perversion and reputable sins like gossip and slander. It includes private sins like haughtiness, social sins like slander, and religious sins like "haters of God." All of these were, in Paul's mind, the visitation of the wrath of God on men who had rebelled against him.

The final step is complete spiritual blindness. Knowing God's "decree that those who do such things deserve to die, they not only do them but approve of those who practice them" (1:32).

Concerning the Gentiles, sin in its essence, the root sin, is rebellion against God and the enthronement of the creature. The fruit sins whether sensual, mental, or spiritual, whether disreputable or reputable, whether private or public, are results of the root sin and are the curse of God.

While Paul is speaking thus, the Judaizer (Paul's straw man in Romans whom he often quotes) is nodding his agreement. He joins Paul in judging the Gentile. But his assent boomerangs.[6] Paul turns upon him and says, "you too are a sinner, you too are without excuse" for "you are doing the very same things" that the Gentile does (2:1). Thus, he rules out all possibility of separating Jews from Gentiles as the Pharisees did. All, not just the Gentiles, are under the wrath of God; all are "under the power of sin" (3:9).

The Jew's root sin lies in his presumption on the goodness of God (2:4). Like the Gentile, he reverses the role of the creature and Creator, but by making God the servant of man. Since he is a Jew, he feels that God is obligated to him, that his goodness is only a sign of this obligation. Instead of seeing God's goodness as an incentive to repent, he presumes upon it. Instead of seeing his circumcision as a call to devotion to God, he remains uncircumcised in heart (2:25–29).

His fruit sins are the same, but different. Instead of armed robbery, he cheats. Instead of idolatry, he blasphemes. Instead of adultery, he has serial marriages. He finds more refined ways of breaking the commandments of God (2:22–24). Not only so, being blind to his own sin, he sets himself up as "a guide to the blind," "a corrector of the foolish, a teacher of children" (2:17-19). But in teaching others, he fails to instruct himself (2:21).

Paul's straw man (the Judaizer) objects. "If what you say is true," he says, "what advantage has the Jew? Or what is the value of circumcision?" (3:1). "Much in every way," Paul replied. "To begin with, the Jews were entrusted with the oracles of God" (3:2). He then sweeps the props from under his opponent by pointing out that possession of the law does not obligate God to bless the unfaithful Jew. Nor does the unfaithfulness of the Jew nullify "the faithfulness of God" (3:3-8).

But "are the Jews any better off?" "No," Paul replies, "not at all. All men, both Jews and Greeks, are under the power of sin" (3:9). The law does not change that. The law only brings knowledge of sin, not knowledge of salvation. "All have sinned, each one for himself, and thus have come short of the glory God intended man to have (3:23, my paraphrase). Thus all are "accountable"; all are "without excuse."

II. Romans 5:12-14

This is a famous passage in Christian debate; it has been greatly overemphasized in discussing Paul's doctrine of sin. Actually the doctrine of sin is not the subject being discussed; Paul is talking about the meaning of the cross. In doing so, he draws a series of comparisons and contrasts between Adam and Christ.

The comparison lies mainly in the fact that both Adam and Christ started something *in the world*. Adam started the process characterized by the words: sin—transgressions—condemnation—death. Christ started the process characterized by the words: grace—free gift—righteousness (i.e., justification)—life. Adam started his process by one act of sin in which he rebelled against God's right to command him. Christ started his by an act of righteousness, that is, his death on the cross. Paul did not mean to equate Adam and Christ as figures of "equal value"; Adam comes before Christ, but only as a shadow and example.[7] The results of Adam's sin stand only as a dark background against which to display the glorious work of Christ.

Even so, the comparison is not exact; there is contrast as well. The contrast is contained in the words "much more" (vv. 15,17,20). "The act of grace does not balance the act of sin; it over-balances it."[8] The saved man is not returned to innocence, only to be subject again to sin and death. He is lifted to a new life, freed from the dominion of sin (Rom. 6:14). Perhaps also the idea of God's delight in mercy is contained in the words "much more." Man can be even more certain that this one

Man's righteousness will result in life than that that one man's sin did result in death.[9]

The problem has been that some scholars have insisted that Paul is attributing "the sin of all men to Adam's sin." This is still the opinion of some New Testament scholars.[10] It has been the opinion of many theologians in the past—both Catholic and Protestant. One standard book on theology takes nearly one hundred pages to discuss the origin of sin in the personal act of Adam, the imputation of Adam's sin to his posterity, and the consequences (i.e., depravity, guilt, and penalty) of sin to Adam's posterity.[11] The dispute has not been on the fact, but on the *rationale*. How could God hold every man responsible for Adam's sin? Two primary explanations have held the field—the seminal and the federal theories. According to the one, we were all actually, *seminally,* that is, in seed, in Adam when he sinned, were thus involved in his sin, and are held guilty of it. According to the other, Adam acted as the federal head of the race, representing all men. Therefore the guilt of his act is racial as well as personal.

This whole debate is misdirected. It seeks to explain something that is not true. No man but Adam is guilty of Adam's sin. No man will be eternally lost apart from his own personal choice and sin. Any other theory is "not interpreting Paul."[12] It is more closely related to pre-Pauline thought than to Paul.[13] Paul, indeed, used an ancient scheme that implied the threat of a fateful destiny for man, but he "reshaped" and "applied it in a totally new way."[14] The whole passage asserts that man is not caught up in fate, a sinner by necessity. The cause of sin is "man's desire to assert his own will against God," the same kind of desire that brought about Adam's ruin.[15] To say this is not to deny the solidarity of the race and the undeniable fact that we often suffer for the sins of others. But suffering is not punishment, even though punishment can sometimes take the form of suffering. Punishment comes because of personal guilt (i.e., desert of punishment, a fact and not a feeling), and guilt is not transferrable.

However, this passage does teach a connection, a mediated connection, between Adam's sin and ours. "Sin came into the world through one man and death through sin, and so death spread to all men because all men sinned" (v. 12). The word "sinned" is in the Greek aorist tense and this has led many scholars to say: "all sinned in Adam's sin." We have noted the impossibility of this. We must give the verb the same meaning here that it has in Romans 3:23 (where it is also aorist): "all sinned personally."

Paul is careful to point out that sin existed before the law was given. The proof of this is that death "reigned from Adam to Moses, even over those whose sins [note: each man had his own kind of sins] were not like the transgression of Adam [i.e., disobedience of an express command of God]" (v. 14). The law was given to turn sin into transgression, that is, to confront man with express commands of God, the breaking of which is transgression.

The context confirms this exegesis. We know that Christ's death results in our salvation, but we know that his death is mediated to us through personal faith. Salvation is not automatic; it must be appropriated by faith. All men are only *potentially* saved by the death of Christ. The same mediation must be implied for the other side of the equation. Adam sinned—following his example, all men individually sinned by personal choice—all men died. The purpose of Paul in writing is not to give a complete account of his doctrine of sin or his doctrine of salvation; it is to point out the decisive importance for human history of the two acts—one of disobedience; one of obedience.

I do not deny that every man is born with an inherent tendency toward self-assertion against God and that he is forced to live in a world which is hostile to God. One may pity man and feel that he is under both internal and external compulsion to sin, but he must not destroy man's humanity by insisting that he is the victim of fate. His sin is by personal choice.

III. Romans 6:20-23

Though not a discussion of sin, this passage says some important things about man's predicament. Paul uses the fact of man's total involvement in sin before salvation to demand the Christian's total commitment to God now. "When you were slaves of sin, you were free in regard to righteousness" (v. 20). Paul saw man, not as one who was partially corrupted by sin, but as one who was totally and completely involved in its practice. Paul believed in "total depravity," not in the sense that all men were morally as evil as possible, but in the sense that every man's total being was under the power of sin.

"The end of those things is death" (v. 21) and "the wages of sin is death" (v. 23). Paul thought of sin as fatal. Death was its end, its wages (i.e., what it earned and brought to man without fail). Of course, he was not using "death" in the modern sense of "physical death." He did not think in our terms. Death, like sin, involved the whole of man. It consisted of total and complete separation from God and good. In the future,

IV. Romans 7:7-25

This passage is a highly dramatic assertion of the futility of the law as a way of salvation. A deadly duel is in process and "I" am the battleground. The protagonists are "the law" and "sin." But even the "I" is divided. The "inner man" (v. 22) seeks to go in one direction; "the flesh" which is also "I" pulls in the other direction (v. 18).

The spiritual odyssey of "I" is sketched in three parts. Part I: "I" was once alive (v. 9), not "knowing sin" (v. 7), although "sin" lay like a sleeping monster within me, ready to spring to life and do me to death (v. 9). Part II: "I" was confronted by the law: "You shall not covet" (v. 7). The law, though "good" (v. 13), gave opportunity to sin, and sin slew me (vv. 8-9). Thus, sin reveals itself in all its horror, able to use the good to accomplish the evil.

Part III: "I" did not give up; "I" struggled. Something within me, "my inner man" (v. 22) urged me to obey the law and win the approval of God. "I" tried, but "I" failed. Something else within me, my human nature (i.e., the flesh) kept me from it. "I" am now a wretched man, held prisoner by this "body of death," crying out for a deliverer (v. 24).

Who is the "I" of this passage? Is he the believer or the unbeliever? Is he Paul himself or the race? Scholars have had a field day with this passage. There is no consensus anywhere.

First, I would agree that the "I" of this passage is the unbeliever, that the chapter describes man under the law, "his existence in the flesh." [16] My primary reason for this conclusion is that the "I" in this passage ends up in hopeless despair. This does not describe the believer who struggles with the power of sin in his own life. A believer has such struggles; Paul recognizes them and describes them (Gal. 5:16-17). But the believer has a deliverer; the Holy Spirit dwells within him; sin's dominion has been ended in him (Rom. 6:12-14). The believer need not despair; he can win the victory. But at every point the unbeliever's case is different. He does not have a deliverer; the Holy Spirit does not dwell with him; sin's dominion has not been broken; he has only his own resources to rely upon; he cannot win the victory.

But is the "I" Paul as a Pharisee? This was once a very popular opinion but is now denied by the majority of scholars.[17] The main reason for denying the identity between "I" and Paul is the statement that Paul never speaks elsewhere of moral despair before his conversion. Rather, he speaks with pride of his blamelessness when judged by the righteousness based on obedience to the law (Phil. 3:6). "His letters reveal no conscious dissatisfaction with his religious life before conversion."[18] This may be true, but Paul's letters were not meant as a psychological self-study; his statements about his blamelessness emphasizes only a fact.

More to the point is Rubenstein's self-study which shows a high degree of conformity accompanied by an inner feeling of frustration. He, a modern Jew, in training for the rabbinate, committed himself to the law but experienced a continuous feeling of inner failure which compelled him to become "ever more scrupulous." But increased scrupulosity did not dispel his anxiety or sense of guilt. God became to him, invented by his imagination, "my never-failing Watchman, Lawgiver, and Judge" —so much so that he came to hate God and wished him dead.[19]

Whether Paul experienced such feelings is debatable. He may have; he may not have. Silence about them is proof for neither opinion. But in this passage, "there is a passion and a poignancy in his words which makes it hard to suppose that he is speaking in the abstract."[20] It is more probable that he makes himself the type of all men.

What does this passage reveal about Paul's doctrine of sin? Much! "Sin" is used in the singular here for a power or force that enslaves man; this is Paul's usual way of speaking of sin. He personifies sin, but he is not thinking of sin as something invading man from the outside. It is a monster within man, dormant until the opportunity arises. Then it revives and slays man. Whether we want to agree or not, Paul felt that the man who was enslaved by sin had no good in him. He says, "For I know that nothing good dwells within me, that is, in my flesh. I can will what is right, but I cannot do it" (v. 18). Sin, to Paul, neither consisted "simply in a moral failure," nor was it an external force robbing man of his power. Sin was man's own culpable act.[21]

V. 2 Corinthians 5:15

This passage is important to our study because it gives a clue to the meaning of sin for Paul. "He died for all," Paul says, "that those who live might *live no longer for themselves* but for him who for their sake died and was raised" (italics mine). Paul saw sin as a life dedicated to self. Self is the center of the sinner's world; self is the circumference of his thoughts; self is his god. This is only another way of saying that the essence of sin is rebellion against God. Man's awful predicament, outside of Christ, is that he has substituted self for God.

VI. Paul's Doctrine of Sin Summarized

Other passages, shorter and not so important, could be studied. These, however, seem to cover all the bases in Paul's thought on the subject of sin, the basis of man's need for salvation. Let us see what the sum of the matter is with Paul.

(1) Sin is rebellion against God. This is the root sin from which all sins spring, the sin-principle which dominates man's life. It is the refusal to acknowledge God's right in man's life. It is not so much transgression of a command as it is the denial of God's right to command. It is the affirmation of self-will over against God's will.[22] It is "perversity of mind rather than debility of the flesh."[23] It is the refusal to let God function as God in man's life, an effort to usurp God's place, to dethrone him.[24] Sin is a state of being, a state of arrogant defiance against the will of God.[25] Sin may manifest itself in man's life in many ways, even an attempt through religious devotion to gain status for oneself before God. This attempt to "preserve independence over against God is the root sin."[26] Sin is not a matter of doing or not doing. It is a matter of being or not being. It is man "falling victim to himself."[27] This condition is man's own choice, not a fate that awaits him. Paul permits no blurring of the lines of personal responsibility.[28]

(2) Sin is universal. Both Jew and Gentile are under its power. "There is no difference: for all have sinned and come short of the glory of God" (Rom. 3:22–23, KJV).

(3) Sin is inexcusable. Paul goes to great lengths to make this point. Both the Jew and the Gentile have sufficient knowledge of God, one from nature and conscience, the other from these plus the law, to make their usurpation of God's place in their lives without excuse. Alike, they are culpable; alike, they are accountable to God. Paul never views sin as due to fate, to inheritance, to social pressures. In his mind, it is always due to personal choice. No more is sin due to man's ignorance or his weakness; it is due to the rebellious exertion of his will against God.

(4) Sin is enslaving. It binds man to himself and makes self-salvation impossible. The law is weak, but its weakness is due to the weakness of flesh (Rom. 8:3).

(5) Sin is corrupting. Man's effort to be independent of God leads him into all kinds of sins. These are an expression of both the root sin and the curse of God's wrath.

(6) Sin is fatal. It brings death and destruction to man. Paul does not dwell on what this means, but he believes it. Death now and death

later is the "wages" of sin.

We must repeat: Paul does not set forth the doctrine of sin for its own sake. He is no sadist, delighting in the frustration and doom of man. He presents it in the interests of the gospel. He wants men to know that their plight is hopeless outside of Christ. He knows that so long as men rely on some other way of salvation, they are doomed. Only when they give up hope can they hope. Only when they throw themselves upon the mercy of God, without any claim on him, is their claim to salvation established.

NOTES

1. Bornkamm, *Paul,* p. 125.   2. Abbott-Smith, *Lexicon,* p. 210.
3. Käsemann, *An Die Römer,* p. 33.   4. Bornkamm, *Paul,* p. 122.
5. *Ibid.*   6. *Ibid.,* p. 123.
7. Karl Barth, *A Shorter Commentary on Romans* (Richmond: John Knox, c. 1959), p. 62.
8. C. K. Barrett, *The Epistle to the Romans* (New York: Harper & Row, c. 1957), p. 113.
9. James Denney, "Romans," *Expositor's Greek Testament,* ed. W. R. Nicoll (Grand Rapids: Eerdman's reprint edition, n. c.), Vol. II, p. 629.
10. Bultmann, *Theology,* V. I, p. 251. cf. Conzelmann, *Outlines,* p. 195.
11. A. H. Strong, *Systematic Theology,* pp. 582–664.
12. W. T. Conner, *Faith,* p. 281.   13. Bornkamm, *Paul,* p. 124.
14. *Ibid.*   15. *Ibid.*
16. Günther Bornkamm, *Early Christian Experience* (London: SCM Press, 1969), p. 89. Cf. Rudolf Bultmann, *The Old and the New Man in the Letters of Paul* (Richmond: John Knox Press, 1967), p. 33.
17. Bultmann, *op. cit.,* p. 33; Schoeps, *Paul,* p. 184; Menoud, "Tradition and Revelation," p. 132; Bornkamm, *Paul,* p. 125.
18. Richard L. Rubenstein, *My Brother Paul* (New York: Harper & Row, 1972), p. 10.
19. *Ibid.*
20. Sidney Cave, *The Gospel of Paul* (Garden City, N.Y.: Doubleday, 1929), p. 36.
21. Bornkamm, *Paul,* p. 126.
22. John A. MacKay, *God's Order* (New York: The Macmillan Co., 1953), p. 89.
23. *Ibid.*   24. Rutenber, *The Reconciling Christ,* p. 45.
25. Wright and Fuller, *God's Acts,* p. 327.
26. Käsemann, *New Testament Questions,* p. 180.
27. Bornkamm, *Paul,* p. 133.   28. Stewart, *A Man in Christ,* p. 107.

6
SALVATION BY GRACE THROUGH FAITH

The key issue in Paul's conflict with the Judaizers was: How are men saved? The Judaizers said, "By grace through faith *plus* circumcision and obedience to the law." Paul said, "By *grace alone* through *faith alone.*" The Judaizers' idea of grace was that of Judaism: God supplies our deficiencies. They thought God exercised tolerant forbearance with those who *really tried* to obey the law. He rejoiced in the good man's efforts. When they fell short, he stepped in and made up the difference.[1] Not so with Paul. Human efforts are worthless; he demanded that all claim to merit be renounced. Grace—grace alone and grace all the way—was the only way of salvation. Faith alone and faith all the way appropriated the salvation grace provided.

Paul's love for antithesis is readily detected even by a casual reader.[2] In Romans 4:1-17, there are five sets of opposites. Promise is the opposite of law. Faith is the opposite of works. Righteousness is the opposite of wrath. Heirs of God is the opposite of being condemned by God. Grace is the opposite of merit. The opposition is radical and mutually exclusive.[3] Grace does not supplement merit; it annuls it. Faith does not supplement works; it excludes them. Promise does not supplement law; it supersedes it. There is no middle ground on which these terms overlap.

I. Grace Acting for Redemption

That God is the only source of salvation is the most persistent accent of biblical thought.[4] It is also the most persistent accent of Paul's thought. Moffatt has noted that "grace" is seldom used in the Gospels, but seldom absent in Paul's writings.[5] Bornkamm insists that Paul has given to the catchwords "by God alone" and "by grace alone" a new and all inclusive meaning.[6] "Grace" is one of the great words in Paul's vocabulary; he used it more than twice as many times as all the rest of the New Testament writers.[7] The use of it, in his letters, is concentrated in the four letters which are most closely related to the Judaizing controversy—Romans, 1 Corinthians, 2 Corinthians, and Galatians.

What did Paul mean by grace? First, it meant God acting in accordance with his own character and being.[8] Grace did not mean a quality or attitude of God; it meant God himself. Paul never rises to John's statement: "God is love" (1 John 4:8), but he would have agreed with it. It was God "who is rich in mercy, out of the great love with which he loved us" that made sinners alive in Christ (Eph. 2:4). The same thought is restated in the words: "by grace you have been saved" (Eph. 2:8). Paul equates the action of God with the action of love and grace. He shows how little he would think of the not uncommon idea that one quality of God—his grace—does battle with another quality—his righteousness—in bringing salvation to man. No, salvation is the act of God—the act of the whole being of God.

Second, grace is always an act in behalf of the unworthy; it is "unmerited favor." It is always thought of as a "free gift" (Rom. 5:15). Paul would not permit any blurring of the lines between grace and works. There could be no compromise. Those who wished to be justified by the law had fallen away from the way of grace (Gal. 5:4). If a thing were by grace, "it is no longer on the basis of works; otherwise grace would no longer be grace" (Rom. 11:6). A "free gift" and "wages" earned were entirely different (Rom. 11:4). Any contribution of man to his own salvation was utterly excluded. God's grace stands in opposition to everything self-made wherein man thinks himself self-sufficient. "Boasting is excluded" (Rom. 3:27).

Third, grace is an act, not an attitude of God. Paul uses the word in the singular and characterizes it as an act, a saving act, which is "pure gift."[9] Perhaps it is too much to say that the word only meant "a single deed," the "deed of divine grace" by which "God gave up Christ to die on the cross."[10] Bultmann bases his conclusions on the undoubted fact that both the "love and "grace" of God are most often connected with the death of Christ by Paul. There can be no doubt that Paul thought of the cross as the supreme gift and manifestation of God's grace. "Grace," however, is often used for other deeds of God in the experience of men.

Fourth, grace is always God acting for salvation. It describes the manward action of God. Redemption is always the end sought by God when he acts in grace. By grace salvation is provided. By grace we are called to salvation. By grace we are enabled to have faith. By grace we are made God's children. By grace we are endued with power and gifts for Christian living and service. By grace we are kept in fellowship with

God. By grace we will enter heaven. The supreme glory of God, in heaven, will be seen in his grace toward us (Eph. 1:6).

Fifth, grace is God acting on purpose. Calvin was right in seeing that an eternal purpose of predestination and election was an essential deduction from the doctrine of grace. If man's salvation is historically conditioned in any way, it is to that degree less than salvation by grace. The reason and impetus and power for salvation must be found in God alone.

Paul does not speak often of God's eternal purpose; he was too engrossed in the working out of that purpose in history. In one chapter (Rom. 9), he speaks of God's purpose and sovereign choice of men and nations in their role in salvation-history. In another (Rom. 8), he speaks of the election of individuals to salvation. "Those whom he foreknew he also predestined to be conformed to the image of his Son. . . . And those whom he predestined he also called; and those whom he called he also justified; and those whom he justified he also glorified" (vv. 29-30).

To define Paul's doctrine of predestination is dangerous, but I will try. It is this: God does what he does *in saving people* on purpose.[11] Paul simply ascribed whatever God did in history to God's eternal purpose. He reasoned that whatever God did he did on purpose. What God did is *salvation*. The purpose of God, *as it touches the individual's life* is limited to salvation. Paul never ascribes the damnation of man to God's purpose. If man were adamant in his sin, how could he accuse God of having predestined him to damnation? Would that Christian theologians through the ages had been so wise!

But when it comes to salvation, Paul was certain that the act of God in history was grounded in his eternal purpose for individual men. His choice was unconditional; it did not rest upon any superiority of the man chosen. His choice was eternal; it did not rest upon historical happenstance. His choice was irreversible; all those chosen would be finally saved.

II. Grace Acting in History

Paul had a theology of history as we have already noted. Being a Jew, this must follow. The idea of a divine purpose being worked out in creation and history is "the great contribution of Hebrew thinkers to the world of thought" as well as the basis of faith and the foundation of monotheism.[12] Being a convert meant that he had seen Christ as the fulfillment and climax of history. But his salvation-history was fragmentary rather than complete. He made no effort to interpret all of history as saving history. No doubt, he looked upon creation as having redemptive ends. At any rate, he saw creation as sharing the "subjection to futility" of sinful men, not by its own choice, but by the will of God (Rom. 8:20). He also felt that creation would "be set free from its bondage to decay and obtain the glorious liberty of the children of God" (Rom. 8:21).

He also recognized the headship of Adam over the human race (Rom. 5:12–14), but he did not see Adam as a part of salvation-history. He saw him as the first man whose sin made salvation necessary. Nor did Paul have much to say about world history in general. Rather, "God's history was a radical countermovement to earthly history.[13]

(1) *Abraham is the beginning of salvation history* for Paul. It was to him that the promises were made which are now being fulfilled in the gospel (Gal. 3:15). He uses rabbinic interpretation of the call of Abraham (Gen. 12:7) as a vehicle to assert that the line of salvation-history goes from Abraham to Christ. The promise was to Abraham and to his seed ("seed" being a collective noun for all the descendants of Abraham). Paul bases his exegesis of the passage on the fact that the Greek word for seed is in the singular. He says the promises were not to Abraham and his "offsprings" as if it referred to many, but to Abraham and his "offspring" which is "Christ" (Gal. 3:16).

Whatever we may think of Paul's exegesis, we must admit that for him the two great epochs of salvation-history were the call of Abraham and the sending of Christ.

In another passage, he uses another line of thought to show that the history of Abraham was a prehistory of salvation by grace through faith. He points to the Scripture passage which says: "Abraham believed God, and it was reckoned to him for righteousness" (Rom. 4:3; cf. Gen. 15:6). He then argues that Abraham's faith preceded his circumcision which he received as a sign or seal of righteousness which he had by faith (Rom. 4:11). This meant that Abraham was the "father of all who believe without circumcision and who thus have the righteousness reckoned to them" (Rom. 4:11).

This means that the "promise" rests on "grace" and is "guaranteed to all his descendants—not only to the adherents of the law but also to those who share the faith of Abraham, for he is the father of us all" (Rom. 4:16). The descent from Abraham, the one that really counts, is not the natural descent of the flesh, but the spiritual descent of faith.

(2) *The law was given a subsidiary place in* the thought of Paul when viewed from the salvation-history perspective. The relation of the law

to the gospel played an important role both in the experience of Paul and in his controversy with the Judaizers. The Greek word for law appears seventy-two times in Romans and thirty-two times in Galatians, but only eighty-seven times in the rest of the New Testament (including the rest of Paul's letters).

Paul said, if the Judaizers are right, "If it is the adherents of the law who are to be the heirs, faith is null and the promise is void" (Rom. 4:14). The law is disqualified from two standpoints: it came four hundred and thirty years after the promise (Gal. 3:17) and it is contradictory to the promise (Gal. 3:18). The law could not annul the promise.

"Why then the law?" cried Paul's opponent (Gal. 3:19). In the immediate context, Paul gives the function of the law in salvation-history. In other contexts, he treats the law from two other perspectives: as the gift of God and as a means to personal salvation. To avoid confusion, we will notice how Paul thought of the law from these two perspectives and return to our discussion of its function in salvation-history.

First, Paul looked upon the law as the gift of God, a blessing beyond measure to Israel. Among the proud possessions of Israel was "the giving of the law" (Rom. 9:4). In it, Israel had "the embodiment of knowledge and truth" (Rom. 2:20). When asked what advantage the Jew had over the Gentile, he said: "Much in every way. To begin with, the Jews were entrusted with the oracles of God" (Rom. 3:2). Paul certainly did not look upon the law as false.[14] It is "holy, and the commandment is holy and just and good" (Rom. 7:12). Thus, the law was still in force as moral demand.[15] This refers to what may be called the ethical demands of the law, not the ritual law.[16]

Because the law is good and its requirements are just, the believer is obligated to "fulfill these demands." He is now able to do so because God has condemned sin through Christ and because the believer no longer walks according to "the flesh but according to the Spirit" (Rom. 8:4). This fulfillment, however, was not thought of as mere legalistic obedience after the manner of the Jews; it was to be a fulfillment in spirit. Paul's recurring emphasis was: "Owe no man anything, except to love one another; for he who loves his neighbor has fulfilled the law" (Rom. 13:8).

Second, from the perspective of personal salvation, the law had been discredited. It was powerless to save.[17] The law indeed promised life to those who practiced it perfectly from the cradle to the grave (Rom. 7:10; 10:5). But the promise is impossible for man; the law has been weakened by the flesh (Rom. 8:3) and has become the "law of sin and death" (Rom.

8:2). Its ministration is a ministration of "death" and "condemnation" (2 Cor. 3:7–9). The "written code kills" (2 Cor. 3:6).

It is important to remember that the reason for the desperate situation of the man under law is not due to the law's inferiority; it does not mediate a false knowledge of God and his will.[18] The situation is desperate because "prior to faith *there is no true fulfillment of the law.*" [19] Paul was drawing on his own experiences in this. "For I through the law died to the law, that I might live to God" (Gal. 2:19). He was adamant in saying that "by works of the law shall no one be justified" (Gal. 2:16). Why? "For all who rely on works of the law are under a curse; for it is written, "Cursed be every one who does not abide by all things written in the book of the law, do them" (Gal. 3:10; cf. Deut. 27:26). Thus, as a way of life, the law stood discredited. It could not even contribute to the saving situation, but "a man is justified by faith apart from works of law" (Rom. 3:28). In saying this, Paul cut the ground out from under his Judaizing opponents who looked upon salvation as coming from faith *plus* keeping the law. No human achievement of any kind can contribute to man's salvation.

Now let us return to our subject. From the salvation-historical perspective, the law played a subordinate role. Paul's discussion is found primarily in Galatians 3:19 to 4:7. "It was added for the sake of transgressions" (Gal. 3:19). The usual translation, "because of transgressions" (RSV) is manifestly wrong. Transgression is the breaking of a specific command; Paul knew that sin existed before the law, but transgressions did not (Rom. 5:13). What then does he means by "for the sake of transgressions"? It cannot be denied that Paul thought that the law led men to sin.[20] "Through the law comes knowledge of sin" (Rom. 3:20), and "I should not have known sin, . . . if the law had not said, 'You shall not covet' " (Rom. 7:7). In both passages, knowledge of sin is practical knowledge, knowing sin as a part of one's experience.[21] This thought belongs, however, to Paul's viewing the law as discredited as a way of salvation.

In the historical perspective one could hardly say that God had given the law to promote sin. No, what he meant was that God had given the law to reveal sin, to bring to light that man is sinful, whether his desire leads him to break the law or, paradoxically, to a zeal for keeping the law.[22] "For the sake of transgressions" means that the law turned the preexisting sins of men into definite offenses against a known commandment.[23] In doing this, it convinces man that he is a sinner.

But the aim of the law in God's eyes was still gospel. It was a temporary expedient.[24] but it did play a historical role.[25] "The writing [i.e., the law] locked up all things together under the power of sin in order that the promise by Faith in Christ might be given to the believers" (Gal. 3:22, my translation). The law is looked upon as a jailer who keeps all things (i.e., all men) locked up under condemnation so that grace may abound in their salvation.

This is also what Paul means when he calls the law *a pedagogue* "until Christ came" (Gal. 3:24). Unfortunately the Greek word has entered the English language to refer to a teaching function. This has led many to think that Paul's meaning here refers to the teaching function of the law. This is not Paul's meaning. The *pedagogue* in the Greek family was a slave in charge of the minor children. The function of the pedagogue was to discipline the children, at home or at school. Thus, the law is not in Paul's mind an educator, but a "task-master." [26] The law disciplines the minor child, that is, historical Israel, until Christ comes and sets the child free. Under another figure the same thought is repeated. The minor child has no more privilege than a slave, he is kept under "guardians and trustees until the date set by the father" (Gal. 4:1–2). In the same way, the Jews were slaves "to the elements of the universe" (literal translation), that is, the law, until the coming of Christ.

The law did function however in the interests of the gospel. God's purpose in it all is that "we might be justified by faith" (Gal. 3:24). This purpose is now seen in the coming of Christ who makes it possible for us to "receive adoption as sons" (Gal. 4:5).

(3) *The place of Israel* was a problem both to Paul and to his opponents. To Paul, it was an emotional problem. To his opponents, it was a theological problem. Both agreed that Israel was God's chosen people. Both agreed that God had blessed and used Israel in preparation for the coming of Christ. "They are Israelites, and to them belong the sonship, the glory, the covenants, the giving of the law, the worship, and the promises; to them belong the patriarchs, and of their race, according to the flesh, is the Christ" (Rom. 9:4–5). This brief summary of Israel's place in God's salvation-history would have elicited an "amen" from the Judaizers.

The problem was that Israel was not in the Christian movement. To Paul, this unbelief of Israel was an emotional problem: "I could wish that I myself were accursed and cut off from Christ for the sake of my brethren, my kinsmen by race" (Rom. 9:3; cf. 10:1). To Paul's opponents, the present exclusion of Israel was a theological problem. How could the gospel be God's true way of salvation if Israel was excluded?

Paul answers the theological problem in a prolonged statement (Rom. 9—11) which to modern scholars seems to be a parenthesis in the book of Romans. Not so to Paul. He recognized the necessity of reconciling the doctrine of universal salvation with the election of Israel.[27] To him and his opponents these chapters are an integral and necessary part of the gospel.

First, he points out that Israel can make no claims on God on the basis of past history and blessings (9:1–24). The exclusion of Israel does not mean that the "word of God had failed" (9:6). Paul is speaking of a "role of history," not of individual salvation. His statments about predestination in this chapter, when applied to individual salvation, have led many astray. The main point is that Israel's past history was based on a divine choice, not on merit. Therefore, since God made Israel, he has the right to do what he will with her, regardless of the past (9:21–24).

Second, the exclusion of Israel from the Christian gospel is not due to God's purpose, but to Israel's own inexcusable unbelief (9:27 to 10:21). God, through the prophets, had spoken of coming salvation. The fact that Israel did not recognize God's working in Christ is due to her hardness of heart, to her attempt to establish self-righteousness instead of accepting the righteousness of God (10:1–4). God cannot therefore be blamed, nor can the gospel be discredited, on the basis of Israel's unbelief. The way is still open to her. Each Israelite who believes will be saved. He has only to confess: "Jesus is Lord" and believe in his heart "that God has raised him from the dead" (Rom. 10:9).

Third, Paul speaks to his problem—the emotional one (11:1–32). He considers that his previous statements have solved the theological problem. The essence of his statement is that the exclusion of Israel is *neither complete nor final.* It is not complete because a believing remnant of Israel, including Paul himself, has believed (11:1–6). This proves that God has not rejected his "people whom he foreknew" (11:2). This conforms to history as well, because only a remnant, a believing and obedient remnant, was accepted in Elijah's day (11:2–5).

The *exclusion is not final* because God will use the inclusion of the Gentiles to bring about the salvation of the Jews (11:7–32). Through the "stumbling" of the Jews "salvation has come to the Gentiles, so as to make Israel jealous" (11:11). Through that jealousy, through the Gentile mission, Paul expects that "all" Israel will someday be saved (11:26). Just how seriously Paul is to be taken here is a subject of long debate. It seems to me that the debate can be solved by reference to Paul's own statements. By Israel, he undoubtedly meant natural Israel, not spiritual

SALVATION BY GRACE THROUGH FAITH   93

Israel. The only place where Paul uses "Israel" in any sense other than natural Israel is in Galatians 6:16 where most interpreters take "the Israel of God" to refer to all believers. Burton argues strongly and convincingly however that the expression means the believing Jews.[28] By "all Israel will be saved," he undoubtedly meant all Jewish believers, whatever their number might be. To seek to find another way for the Jews to be saved does violence to the whole New Testament. Paul never suggested that Israel could be saved except by grace through faith. They must individually be grafted back into the tree of salvation.

This is Paul's answer to the Judaizers concerning the role of Israel. Her role has been great; her election has been validated. *As a nation,* she has become an "outsider" in God's redemptive program because of her unbelief. *As individuals,* she is still the object of God's concern, invited to sit in on the riches of salvation, and this will surely lead to her ultimate salvation.

(4) Christ is *the climactic element in salvation history.* He is the "end" of the law (Rom. 10:4), an expression which in the light of Galatians 3:24 must mean the "goal of the law." It was toward Christ that the law pointed and toward him that it moved men. His coming means that the purpose of God in the law has been accomplished. He is the goal of all of Israel's history. "When the time had fully come, God sent forth his Son, born of a woman, born under the law, . . . so that we might receive adoption as sons" (Gal. 4:4–5). The end, that is, the goal, of the ages has already been reached. We Christians are the ones "upon whom the end of the ages has come" (1 Cor. 10:11). In this sense, the Christian age is the eschatological age, Christ is the midpoint of God's salvation-history. The point toward which the past flowed; the point from which the future flows.[29]

(5) Christ is the midpoint of salvation history, but *not its completion.* According to Paul, God is still working in history in his churches and his commissioned servants. Paul himself "was made a minister according to the gift of God's grace which was given me by the working of his power" (Eph. 3:7). He, as well as his fellow workers, must be judged as servants of Christ and "stewards of the mysteries of God" (1 Cor. 4:1). He looked upon the Christian assemblies as the primary means by which God channeled his grace into the world in this age.

Also history would have its final consummation in the second advent of Christ and the blessedness of God's children in heaven. Paul considered the future as being the working out of the achievements of Christ in the past. The second advent would not introduce a new dimension to grace; it would only bring to final fruition the dimension introduced by the cross.

III. Grace Acting in the Cross

There can be no doubt that the cross was the center of the gospel for Paul.[30] Through his experience, the cross had been transformed "from the wooden instrument of the traitor's death to the supreme altar of the Christian faith."[31] He speaks of the death of Christ over sixty times in Romans, 1 and 2 Corinthians, and Galatians. Usually, but not always, he speaks of the resurrection in the same context. He did not preach a dead Christ but a living Christ who had been crucified. However, in only one passage (Rom. 4:25), and that a part of a pre-Pauline formula, is saving significance assigned to the resurrection. In all other passages, it is the death of Christ and that alone which procures salvation for man. To the Corinthians, he said, "I decided to know nothing among you except Jesus Christ and him crucified" (1 Cor. 2:2). For Paul, the message of the gospel was simply the "word of the cross," folly to the perishing but the power of God to those who are saved (1 Cor. 1:18).

He viewed the cross as an act of God's grace. It was God's act as well as Christ's. There was no attempt to separate a just God from the loving Christ and make the cross an effort to propitiate a reluctant God. Rather, "God was in Christ reconciling the world to himself" (2 Cor. 5:19). God's love is manifested in that "while we were yet sinners Christ died for us" (Rom. 5:8).[32] The continuing provision of God's grace for Christian living is guaranteed by the fact that "He did not spare his own Son but gave him up for us all" (Rom. 8:32). Christ "gave himself for our sins to deliver us from this present evil age" but this was "according to the will of our God and Father" (Gal. 1:4). The cross was an expression of the "vast, unforgettable purpose—the love of God."[33]

At the same time, but without contradiction, the cross could be thought of as cruel murder by the "rulers of this age" (1 Cor. 2:8) or as the self-sacrifice of Christ (Rom. 5:19; Gal. 2:20). Looked at from one viewpoint, the cross was the divine love and grace acting for the salvation of men.[34] This could be spoken of in two ways. Either it is God the Father giving his Son, or it is the Son giving himself. Looked at from another viewpoint, the cross was the "rulers of this age" acting in sin to murder the Son of God. One way of looking at the cross did not detract from the truth of the other, but, for Paul, the emphasis lay clearly on the cross as an act of divine love.

To Paul, the cross was a vicarious act of grace. Christ did not die for himself but for the benefit of others. Christ died for the ungodly (Rom. 5:6), us sinners (Rom. 5:8), us all (Rom. 8:32), the weaker brother (Rom. 14:15), for you (i.e., the Corinthians) (1 Cor. 1:13), you (1 Cor. 11:24), all men (2 Cor. 5:15), for our sake (2 Cor. 5:21), and, most wonderful of all, for me (Gal. 2:20). Paul uses no expression which specifically calls the death of Christ a substitutionary death, but one statement implies it strongly (Gal. 3:13).[35] However, there is little doubt that he thought of it in those terms. The death of Christ was the death I should have died, the death I deserved.

The cross was a victorious act of grace. It accomplished results; it changed the situation between man and God. Paul used various and seemingly inconsistent ways of expressing how Christ fulfilled the office of Messiah. He seized upon any possible expression in his environment and used any terms available to him.[36] Essentially when speaking of the effect of the cross, Paul took two directions.

First, he spoke of what *the death of Christ accomplished* for sinful men. It brings justification (Rom. 3:24; 5:9, 18–19; 2 Cor. 5:21; Gal. 2:21); reconciliation (Rom. 5:10; 2 Cor. 5:18–19), death to the law (Rom. 8:4); salvation (1 Cor. 1:21); the founding of the new covenant (1 Cor. 11:25); deliverance from this present evil age (Gal. 1:4); deliverance from the curse of the law (Gal. 3:13); redemption and adoption as sons (Gal. 4:5); and by it "the world has been crucified to me, and I to the world" (Gal. 6:14). There is no blessing the Christian receives which is not his because of the cross of Christ.

Second, he spoke of the *Godward* meaning of the cross. Paul used a number of figures to indicate how the death of Christ opened the way for the love of God to flow into the hearts of men. The cross was a ransom for men enslaved in sin (Rom. 3:24); "you were bought with a price" (1 Cor. 6:20; 7:23). It was a demonstration of God's righteousness; it showed how God could be righteous and forgive sins—both in the past and in the present (Rom. 3:26). God could not simply overlook sins and remain God. Sin, in all its seriousness must be dealt with. An expiation (or propitiation) was needed. Man had none to make. God furnished one by putting Christ forward "as an expiation by his blood, to be received by faith" (Rom. 3:25). Sacrificial terms are also used.[37] "He died to sin, once for all" (Rom. 6:10); "Christ died for our sins" (1 Cor. 15:3, cf. 2 Cor. 5:21; Gal. 1:4).

In spite of this variety in ways of speaking of the cross, Paul never attempted to "explain it." He had no theory of atonement by which he sought to trace the cause-effect relation between the cross and our salvation.[38] Numerous theologians have tried to construct such a theory. Usually they have laid hold of one aspect of the cross and emphasized this to the exclusion of the other. Their sin has not been that their theory of atonement was false but that it was inadequate to "explain" the cross. I am convinced that this will always be true. The cross cannot be "explained"; it remains a mystery of grace.

But Paul had no doubt about the effectiveness of the cross. Whether we understand it or not, it works. Because Christ died, we live. Because Christ died, God saves.[39] "We were reconciled to God by the death of his Son" (Rom. 5:10). Because this is true, the pretensions of the law are discredited (Gal. 2:21), the rule of God is established in believing hearts (Rom. 3:31), and the Christian is moved to righteous living (2 Cor. 5:14–15). "Despair ends on the cross of Jesus." [40]

To say this is to state the scandal of the Christian gospel to many. We are saying that something of eternal consequence took place in time, that something with heavenly meaning took place on earth. It is difficult for men to see how this can be so, but it must be defended. Philosophers are willing to admit that Jesus revealed God's love on the cross. But, according to Paul, he did far more than that. He did more than reveal God's displeasure with sin; he destroyed the power of sin to enslave and kill. He did far more than reveal the weakness of death; he overcame death. He did far more than reveal God's willingness to forgive sin; he made it possible for God to forgive.

IV. Grace Acting Through Faith

"For I am not ashamed of the gospel: it is the power of God for salvation to every one who has faith, to the Jew first and also to the Greek. For in it the righteousness of God is revealed through faith and for faith; as it is written, 'He who through faith is righteous shall live' " (Rom. 1:16–17). This is the manifesto of Paul with which he introduces the book of Romans. Let us get our prepositions right. We are not saved *by* faith, but *through* faith (Eph. 2:8). The saving power is God's, not man's. It is God acting in grace that saves; faith becomes the complement of grace, the channel through which grace enters the heart and life of man. What was Paul's doctrine of faith?

1. *Faith Is the One Essential to Salvation*

God does not save every Tom, Dick, and Harry but rather "those who, though sinful, yet stand in a certain relationship to Jesus." [41] That relationship is expressed, for Paul, by the word "faith." It is through faith

SALVATION BY GRACE THROUGH FAITH

that what God has done in Christ becomes a "power" in the life of a man.[42] Faith is usually faith in Christ, though occasionally faith in God. The two concepts are not contradictory; faith in Christ is faith in God, and faith in God is faith in Christ.[43]

Paul occasionally uses other terms to express the content of faith. He uses repentance (Rom. 2:4; 2 Cor. 7:9–10), confession that Jesus is Lord (Rom. 10:9–10; Phil. 2:10–11), and obedience to the gospel (Rom. 10:16–17) or to the truth (Gal. 5:7). These expressions are synonyms for faith, but faith best expressed for Paul the radical decision which God demanded of man.

"Repentance," the word which Jesus usually used to speak of decision, was too weak a word in the Greek world to be a vehicle of communication. In the Greek world, repentance never suggested a transformation of character, but only a change of attitude toward some particular opinion or activity.[44] Jesus could use the word because the Hebrew usage implied a complete change of character and disposition, the reversal of the whole course of human behavior, and the turning of the whole man from some other attachment to obedience to God.[45]

But for Paul, in his context, faith must be the word. For him faith is the whole of Christianity subjectively just as Christ is the whole of it objectively. Faith cannot be supplemented or eked out. Every Christian experience depends on faith.[46] Through faith man is saved (Rom. 1:16), receives the righteousness of God (Rom. 3:22), is justified (Rom. 3:28; Gal. 2:16), is forgiven and has his sins covered (Rom. 4:7), obtains access into grace (Rom. 5:1), lives (Gal. 2:20), becomes a son of Abraham (Gal. 3:7), is blessed with Abraham (Gal. 3:9), receives the Spirit which had been promised (Gal. 3:14), and is made a son of God (Gal. 3:26).

Not only is faith essential now; it has always been the way to fellowship with God. Abraham was justified by faith quite as much as Paul was (Rom. 4:3); so also was David (Rom. 4:6–8).[47] Here a misunderstanding must be avoided. It is often said that men of the Old Testament looked forward to the coming of Christ and had faith in the cross while Christians look back to the cross and have faith in it. This is wrong. Neither the faith of Abraham nor the faith of the Christian is faith in a historical event. God, or God in Christ, is the only object of faith. Abraham's faith looked up to God; God looked forward to the cross and saved Abraham on credit. My faith looks up to God; God looks back on the cross and saves me on the basis of what Christ did once for all. I may also look back on the cross and come to appreciate God's grace more fully, but this is not faith. Faith looks to God; it is a personal attitude toward a person.

Thus, for Paul, faith was the word which best expressed the content of man's decision. Without faith one could not be saved; he could not keep the law; he could not have hope. Through faith he could be saved; he could keep the righteous requirement of the law; he could have fellowship with God. In human experience, faith is the continental divide that separates the old life from the new.

2. *Faith Is the Gift of God*

A paradox? If one thing is clear in the thought of Paul, it is that man must decide, that salvation cannot be imposed on man. Those who do not have faith are condemned; they are held responsible for their unbelief (Rom. 9:30–32). When the Christian has been saved, he is conscious that there was a point when he had to say yes when he might have said no.[48] Faith to Paul means *a decision* of the individual man.[49]

On the other hand, Paul is just as clear in his assertion that faith is the gift of God—that man is unable in and of himself to have faith in Christ.[50] The believer is just as conscious that "it is all of God's doing" as he is that he made a decision.[51] Paul said to the Philippians, "It has been granted to you that . . . you should . . . believe in him" (Phil. 1:29). "Granted" is a form of the Greek word from which we get our word "grace." Paul meant to say that the Philippians' faith was a gift of God's grace. In speaking to the Corinthians about the relationship between his own ministry and that of Apollos, he said that he had planted, Apollos had watered, but it was God who was giving "the increase" (1 Cor. 3:6). As a result the Corinthians were "God's field, God's building" (1 Cor. 3:9). This can mean nothing less than that the faith of the Corinthians rested "in the power of God" (1 Cor. 2:5).

After speaking of the death of Christ and the existence of the believer "in Christ," Paul said, "All this is from God" (2 Cor. 5:18). Paul was arrested by God when he revealed his Son "to me" (Gal. 1:15–16). He had been apprehended by Christ (Phil. 3:12). Salvation was by grace through faith, "and this not of your own doing, it is the gift of God" (Eph. 2:8). The antecedent of "this" is the whole process of salvation, including the faith through which it comes. The whole thing is the gift of God.[52] We are not able to make the kind of response to God's grace that is adequate for salvation.[53]

Another way of arriving at the same conclusion is through the Pauline use of "called." "Those whom he predestined he also called; and those whom he called he also justified; and those whom he justified he also glorified" (Rom. 8:30). "Calling" is primarily used by Paul with reference to salvation;[54] it means "effectual calling."[55] "Calling" in the sense in which Paul uses it cannot fail or remain ineffectual.[56] Paul believed that the invitation to salvation was accompanied in the case of those who responded in faith with an inward and effectual "calling," produced directly by the contact of man with God.[57] Paradoxical? Yes. But whether we can understand how faith can be both the decision of man and the gift of God, we must accept the idea as a teaching of Paul. The Christian should be able to understand it. In Christian service, we are aware that what we do is not really our own doing but the work of God within us. At the same time, we are conscious that we are never more ourselves than when we yield ourselves to God as instruments of his righteousness. In the same way, faith is the act of man and the work of God. Faith is not something which the sinner "does." It is rather the recognition that he cannot do anything. It is getting self out of the way so God can do for the sinner what needs done.[58] Manson has suggested that salvation consists of a certain amount of give and take. "God gives and man takes." Salvation is absolutely and entirely the gift of God. *Nothing* that man can do can contribute in the smallest way to the gift. "All that man can do . . . is to take what God gives."[59]

3. Faith Is Not a Work

"Now to one who works, his wages are not reckoned as a gift but as his due. And to one who does not work but trusts him who justifies the ungodly, his faith is reckoned as righteousness" (Rom. 4:4–5). "That is why it depends on faith, in order that the promise may rest on grace" (Rom. 4:16). In these words, Paul states that faith is the very opposite of attempting to win salvation by works. There is a kind of thinking that turns faith into a virtue, that says that the believer merits salvation on the ground of his faith. To say this is to contradict Paul's doctrine of justification.[60] Faith is the opposite of works; faith and works cannot be mixed (Rom. 3:28). This is why justification by faith excludes all boasting (Rom. 3:29). This is why Paul considered the Galatians "bewitched." They had received salvation by "the hearing of faith"; they thought to complete it by "works of flesh" (Gal. 3:1–3).

4. The Content of Faith for Paul

Paul never defines faith.[61] He did not need to. It was a common word in Greek life and its meaning when applied to Christ would be easily understood. "Faithful" was the common way of describing a loyal citizen of a Greek city-state or the adherent of a king. He who was faithful had given his allegiance, wholehearted, and without reserve to that which was sovereign over him. All that was needed was to transfer the meaning to Christ. Faith meant yielding allegiance, wholehearted, and without reserve to Christ.

Unfortunately, we moderns are not so fortunate. The meaning of biblical faith is not clear to us. Too often faith is equated with believing something is true. It is the acceptance of a dogma rather than the yielding of allegiance to a person. We must therefore search for clues in Paul's letters that will help us to understand what he means by faith. What has been said will help. Since the object of saving faith is always a person, faith must be personal rather than theological or mechanical. Since it is the opposite of work, it must be located in the realm of attitude and relationship. Actually, faith, in Paul as well as in John, consists of a combination of three elements.

(1) *The first element is heart belief.* "Faith comes by hearing" (Rom. 10:17). Justification comes by the hearing that is accompanied by faith (Gal. 3:2). This means that there must be a theological foundation to faith. Faith is not a blind leap into the dark; an unquestioning step into the unknown. It is faith in Jesus Christ as preached in the gospel.

Paul said, "If you . . . believe in your heart that God raised him from the dead, you will be saved" (Rom. 10:9). One thing is clear "believing" is an essential element in faith. But it is not mere intellectual belief; it is "heart" belief. It is the kind of belief which appropriates the act of God personally. It is seeing the Son of God as one "who loved *me* and gave himself for *me*" (Gal. 2:20).[62] Faith discerns that Jesus is one worthy of wholehearted allegiance; it sees the act of God in Jesus as directed to *me*. This raises the gospel out of the realm of the purely theological and puts it on the plane of the personal.

(2) A second essential element of faith is *trusting God with ourselves*. "For we are the circumcision, which worship God in the spirit, and rejoice in Christ Jesus, and have no confidence in the flesh" (Phil. 3:3, KJV). The important element in this verse is the phrase "and put no confidence in the flesh" (RSV). Man is forced either to put confidence in his own flesh, what he can accomplish and achieve in and of himself, or to put his confidence in something outside himself. For Paul, the only *trustworthy* one was God and his grace. Faith meant renouncing any achievement of the flesh as Paul had done when he turned his back on his fleshly advantages (Phil. 3:7). It meant putting oneself in the hands of God to do with him what God will.

Notice that it is "trusting self to God" not "trusting God." There is a difference. Some people seem to think they can trust God to save them without submitting their lives to him. What nonsense! Salvation is something that happens *to* you; it is not something God does *for* you. It is *you* who need saving, not your status, your reputation, or even your future. God can save us only when he has us, only when we abandon ourselves to him without reserve, condition, or limit. Such trust may be an act of an instant in its beginning; it must become an attitude of life.

(3) *The capstone of faith is surrender.* "Jesus is Lord" (Rom. 10:9; Phil. 2:11) is one of the oldest, if not the oldest, expressions of Christian faith.[63] In the Christian assembly, such a confession was unmistakably recognized as the work of the Holy Spirit (1 Cor. 12:3).[64] The whole content of faith is summarized in this short formula. Faith is the reversal of the rebellious dissatisfaction of Adam [65] and the willingness to become what we really are, a creature existing "under God."

When we receive Christ, we do not receive him as Savior but as Lord (Col. 2:6). He becomes our Savior when and because he is our Lord. Paul speaks of the "obedience of faith" (Rom. 1:5). This meant for Paul that he was calling the Gentiles to an obedience to God which was faith.[66] "Obedience is as vitally and indissolubly united to faith as breathing is to life." "Faith is first and foremost obedience"; [67] it is acknowledging God's right to command us and our purpose to obey his commands.[68]

Faith, in Paul's mind, was no halfway measure; it contained obedience at its heart.[69] Faith is a committal to God, a committal in which man can make no resolutions of his own. It is a radical decision of the will in which man delivers himself up to God. It is an act of the will in which man negates his own will.[70]

This, then, is what faith meant to Paul. Faith was a good word for him to use to express this vital content of thought. It is not so good today. We may have to find other words to express the content of the gospel in our own day. Bornkamm accuses modern men of repeating the words of another day without understanding their meaning.[71] It is, after all, the meaning that must be preserved, not the words.

NOTES

1. Conzelmann, *Outline,* p. 214.   2. Buck and Taylor, *Saint Paul,* p. 88.
3. *Ibid.*
4. Paul S. Minear, "The Hope of Salvation, *Interpretation,* July, 1949, p. 261.
5. James Moffatt, *Grace in the New Testament,* p. 8.

6. *Paul,* p. 140.   7. Mitter, "Grace," IDB 2, p. 463.
8. *Ibid.,* p. 466.   9. Conzelmann, *Outline,* p. 213.
10. Bultmann, *Theology,* I, pp. 289–292; cf. Bornkamm, *Paul,* p. 141.
11. Fred L. Fisher, *God's Purpose and the Christian's Life* (Philadelphia: Westminster Press, 1962), pp. 113–128.
12. A. C. Wickenden, "Rightly Dividing the Word of Truth," JBL, Jan, 1956, p. 5.
13. Bornkamm, *Paul,* p. 199.   14. Conzelmann, *Outline,* p. 224.
15. *Ibid.*   16. Bultmann, *Theology,* I, p. 260.
17. Stewart, *A Man in Christ,* p. 262.   18. Bultmann, *Theology,* I, p. 262.
19. *Ibid.,* p. 263.   20. Stewart, *op. cit.,* p. 112.
21. Bultmann, *Theology,* I, p. 264.   22. *Ibid.,* p. 265.
23. Burton, *Galatians,* p. 188.   24. Stewart, *op. cit.,* p. 113.
25. Cf. Manson, *On Paul and John,* p. 20.   26. Conzelmann, *Outline,* p. 227.
27. B. W. Helfgott, *The Doctrine of Election in Tannaitic Literature,* (New York: King's Crown Press, 1954), p. 22.
28. *Op. cit.,* p. 358.
29. The discussion is purposely brief here. It has been mentioned before and will be expanded in our discussion of the cross.
30. Barclay, *The Mind of St. Paul,* p. 97; Conner, *Faith,* p. 311.
31. H. Wheeler Robinson, *The Christian Experience of the Holy Spirit,* (London: Nisbet & Co., 1928), p. 78.
32. Conner, *Faith,* p. 311.
33. J. B. Phillips, *Making Men Whole* (New York: Macmillan, 1953), p. 42.
34. Conner, *Faith,* p. 312.   35. Conner, *op. cit.,* p. 317.
36. John Knox, *Chapters in the Life of Paul,* p. 134.
37. Wright and Fuller, *Acts,* p. 34.   38. *Ibid.,* p. 238.
39. W. L. Walker, *The Doctrine of Reconciliation* (Edinburgh: T. & T. Clark, 1908), p. 43; James Denney, *The Christian Doctrine of Reconciliation,* (New York: George H. Doran, Co., c. 1918), p. 327; Phillips, *op. cit.,* p. 38.
40. Käsemann, *Perspectives,* p. 45.   41. Manson, *op. cit.,* p. 58.
42. Conner, *Faith,* p. 253; Wright and Fuller, *Acts,* p. 336; cf. Fitzmeyer, *Pauline Theology,* p. 64.
43. Conner, *Faith,* p. 354; Wright and Fuller, *op. cit.,* p. 337.
44. Manson, *op. cit.,* pp. 58–59.   45. *Ibid.,* p. 59.
46. Denney, *op. cit.,* p. 291.   47. Conner, *Faith,* p. 354.
48. Mitten, *op. cit.,* p. 466.   49. Käsemann, *Perspectives,* p. 83.
50. Barrett, *First Adam to Last,* p. 103.   51. Mitten, *op. cit.,* p. 466.
52. Manson, *op. cit.,* p. 59.
53. Vincent Taylor, *Atonement in the New Testament* (London: Epworth Press, 1941), p. 196.
54. Akira Stake, "Apostolat and Gnade Bei Paulus," NTS, 15, p. 96.
55. Denney, *Romans,* p. 652.
56. William A. Stevens, "II Thessalonians," *American Commentary,* ed. A. Hovey, (Philadelphia: American Baptist Pub. Soc., 1887) V., p. 95.
57. *Ibid.,* p. 95.   58. Conner, *Faith,* p. 356.
59. *Op. cit.,* p. 63.   60. *Ibid.*
61. Bornkamm, *Paul,* p. 141.   62. Phillips, *op. cit.,* p. 40.
63. Barrett, *Romans,* p. 200.
64. Norbert Brox, *Understanding the Message of Paul* (University of Notre Dame Press, c. 1968), p. 47.
65. Barrett, *From First Adam to Last,* p. 103.
66. Karl Barth, *Commentary on Romans,* p. 16.
67. H. R. Mackintosh, *Christian Experience of Forgiveness* (New York: Harper, 1927), p. 153.
68. Brox, *op. cit.,* p. 80.   69. Conner, *Faith,* p. 353.
70. Bultmann, TDNT,   71. Bornkamm, *Paul,* p. 115.

7
LIFE IN CHRIST

What is the meaning of salvation? What happens to a man when he yields his allegiance to Christ? Paul had a problem in trying to express the meaning of salvation. There were no words, certainly not one word, which had content enough to be used. He needed to communicate to others what it meant to be saved. In order to do so, he adopted a variety of terms—justification, reconciliation, sanctification, adoption, salvation, redemption, new creation, and others. These terms came from the law courts, the slave markets, the temples, and other areas of human life.

Paul did not mean that man when he was saved was justified *and* reconciled *and* sanctified *and* adopted. Each term was used for *the whole of salvation's meaning*. When a man looks at a house from the front, he looks at the whole house. Also he looks at the whole house if he looks at it from the back or the sides, from the basement or the roof. Only when he has looked at it from all angles, inside and outside, is the man able to have a clear understanding of the house.

The same thing is true in theology. When one looks at sin, at man, at salvation, at God, at Christ, or at the church, he looks at it from different viewpoints. From one viewpoint, he uses one word to describe what he sees. From another viewpoint, he uses another word. But in each instance he is looking at the reality as a whole. This is the way Paul writes. In one circumstance, one word is used; in another circumstance, another word is used. He means the same thing by both words, but *not exactly the same thing*. Rather, he is describing the same reality from different points of view. Only by looking at the reality from all possible points of view can one have a clear understanding of the totality.

In its simplest terms, salvation is the undoing of sin's damage. It is the reversal of man's whole situation in life. To say this is not enough. Salvation does not just counteract sin; it more than counteracts it. By salvation, man is not just a conqueror of sin; he is a super-conqueror.

Since sin affects the whole of man's life—his relationship with God, his own being, his hope for the future, and his relationship with others, the meaning of salvation must be studied along the same lines.

In the discussion that follows, I have assigned certain of Paul's terms as indicative of man's new relationship with God and certain others as indicative of the new self. In doing this, I violate my own canon. Each term *implicitly* includes the whole meaning of salvation for Paul. But it is true also that each term looks at the total from a particular viewpoint. My division is meant to indicate the primary viewpoint from which salvation is viewed when each separate term is used.

I. Salvation Means a New Relationship with God

Sin makes God and man enemies; it destroys the relationship of creature and Creator. We turn first to those terms which emphasize the new fellowship with God that salvation creates. The primary terms are justification, reconciliation, sanctification, adoption, and in Christ.

1. Justification

Justification has been considered the center of Paul's theology, his favorite way of expressing the believer's new relationship with God. So far as Romans and Galatians are concerned, it is. The idea of justification (expressed either by the verb, the noun, or the prepositional phrase, "righteousness of God" is found a total of fifty times (thirty-nine in Romans and eleven in Galatians). Strikingly, it is found very rarely in the rest of Paul's epistles and hardly at all in the rest of the New Testament.

Justification was "a fighting doctrine," directed against his opponents in the conflict with the Judaizers.[1] It seems that Paul took one of their own words and turned it against them. By its use, he sought to discredit their teaching and establish his in the minds of his churches. We do not know just how the Judaizers preached. It is probable that they followed the teachings of Judaism at this point. If so, two distinctions can be made between Paul's doctrine and theirs. First, Paul believed that justification was a *now* thing, a gift experienced in the present. The Judaizers believed that it was a future thing, realized only at the last judgment.[2] Second, Paul preached that justification came through faith. His favorite way of putting it was: "God counted faith for righteousness." The Judaizers believed, like Judaism, that justification comes through obedience to the law.[3] Unlike Judaism, the Judaizers would add that justification came through faith in Christ *plus* obedience to the law.

What did Paul mean by justification? Answering this question is made difficult by centuries of theological debate. The term is from the law courts. A man was justified if the charges made against him were proved false and he was acquitted. Some theologians, starting from this definition of the term and ignoring the peculiar standpoint from which Paul starts, have insisted that the term must be shut up within legal analogies.[4] They have limited the meaning of the term to: "pronounce righteous," making the gift of God a sort of legal fiction. Usually such scholars have insisted that justification is only one aspect of salvation, that it is accompanied by regeneration which gives the salvation experience an ethical content as well as a formal one.

Others, more superficially still, have thought of justification as a kind of transference of the righteousness of Christ to the believer. Thus the believer, while still unrighteous, stands before God dressed in the righteousness of Christ. This interpretation flies in the face of the fact that Paul nowhere says that we receive the righteousness of Christ. Paul says faith—our faith—is counted for righteousness.

If we study Paul's language in its own contexts, we find the following things to be true with reference to his use of justification:

First, justification is an act of God's grace; it is pure gift. It does not depend in any way on the works or merit of the man justified (Rom. 3:24; 4:1–5; 5:16; 8:33). This is supported by the fact that it is the Gentiles (Rom. 9:30), the "ungodly" (Rom. 4:5), and "sinners" (Rom. 5:8) who are justified.

Second, justification is a present experience of the believer. Paul could say that we "have been justified" (Rom. 5:1).

Third, justification is based upon the redemptive work of Christ on the cross; the justified "are justified by his grace as a gift, through the redemption which is in Christ Jesus" (Rom. 3:24).

Fourth, justification is given only to those who have faith (Rom. 1:17; 3:22, 28). When we ask, "Why faith?" answers differ. Some would say that there is no vital relation between faith and justification. Faith is made the way of justification by the declaration of God. This answer won't do! Faith is reckoned for righteousness because it is righteousness in germ, in embryo. Thus God, who gave faith to begin with, can righteously accept it for what it is not but what it is in seed—true righteousness. This is what saves Paul's doctrine from being a "legal fiction." I would agree that God's gift "must be something more real than a forensic judgment."[5] As Vincent Taylor has said, "If through faith a man is accounted righteous it must be because in some reputable sense he *is* righteous."[6] The sense is in the fact that faith is the beginning of righteousness. Righteousness, in Paul's thought, is a power.[7] It lays hold of the believer as a gift of power enabling him to live a life of righteousness.[8]

Fifth, justification is synonymous with other terms which are definitely dynamic. Paul calls it "justification of life" (Rom. 5:18, KJV). Thus, for Paul, justification denotes a dynamic, life-changing experience.

Paul took a legal word, adopted it, transformed its meaning, and made it the vehicle of his whole thought concerning the initial experience of the Christian life. For him, it meant the act of God's grace by which the sinner is forgiven and received into God's favor and fellowship.[9] It meant everything that is vital in that relation. It meant the revolution of man's whole self, wrought by the power of God. It denotes the entrance into man's life of the power of righteousness by which victory is won over sin, death, and the law. His doctrine of justification is "vital," "positive," "dynamic," and "creative."

2. Reconciliation

Another term Paul uses to express what God does in saving us is reconciliation.[10] This word is found only in Paul's letters. It is used for salvation in Romans and 2 Corinthians only.

The word itself means to make or restore friendship between those who are estranged. The common meaning of the word is found in the passage that speaks of the reconciliation of an estranged husband and wife (1 Cor. 7:10–12).

Paul's use of the word indicates that salvation makes God and man friends. Prior to salvation, sin had made them enemies. A complete reversal has taken place in the relation between God and man. Before salvation, men had been enemies of God (Rom. 5:10) which can mean that they were hostile toward God (Rom. 8:7) or that God hated them (Rom. 5:10; 11:28).[11] The estrangement was mutual; the reconciliation is mutual. It indicates a change in man's attitude toward God and in man's situation before God.

Of course, it is God who has reconciled man to himself. God is the actor; man is the recipient. God takes the initiative. He is the only one who can act in this situation.[12] This fact has misled many scholars into thinking that the result of reconciliation is not a mutual matter, that it speaks only of man's changed attitude toward God and not of man's situation before God (being under God's wrath and judgment). Stewart, for instance, argues almost vehemently that reconciliation is one-sided, that it refers only to a change in man's attitude toward God. He insists that any other opinion is unchristian.[13] He misses the point. In order to preserve the idea of God's initiative in breaking down the barriers, he ignores the fact that the barrier of sin is a barrier to God as well as man.

As with justification, reconciliation is explicitly related to the death of Christ (Rom. 5:6–9; 2 Cor. 5:19). As a matter of fact, the word is used in the Greek Old Testament only in the sense of making an atonement for sins. Paul uses it also in that sense (2 Cor. 5:19). But he also, as noted, uses it in the sense of the subjective results of that atonement—the new fellowship and friendship between God and man. As with justification, reconciliation is also viewed as a completed act, not as a process. "We were reconciled . . . we are reconciled . . . we have now received our reconciliation" (Rom. 5:10–11).

Justification and reconciliation are substitute terms. Making reconciliation means "not counting their trespasses against them" (2 Cor. 5:19).[14] This makes it clear that justification, in Paul's mind, primarily described the new relationship with God which salvation brings or is.

3. Sanctification

It will surprise some to find this word used to describe what happens to man when he becomes a Christian. Too often, and contrary to Paul's usage, sanctification has been looked upon as a sort of second work of grace "superimposed" on justification [15] or as a word describing the growth of the Christian in Christlikeness. The first meaning is never found in the New Testament; the second may be found but only rarely (cf. 1 Thess. 3:13; 4:3–4; 5:23; Rom. 6:19, 22).[16] The confusion is multiplied when the cognate word "saint" is used. In modern usage, a saint is a dead person of unusual religious character or a living person who is especially religious and righteous. With Paul every Christian was a saint; he uses the plural "saints" as his most common word to describe the new Israel, the people of God, who are the Christian believers, whether Jews or Gentiles (1 Cor. 1:2).

The prevalent use of the word by Paul is to describe, not a process, but a completed act of God in which the believer is made into "God's man." God has made Christ Jesus our "wisdom, . . . sanctification, and redemption" (1 Cor. 1:30). The Corinthians had been "washed," "sanctified," and "justified" in the name of Christ (1 Cor. 6:11). Obviously the three words are synonyms; they point to the same experience with slightly different emphases.

The fundamental idea of the term is consecration or dedication. In the Old Testament men and things were "holy" because they had been dedicated to God's service; they belonged to him.[17] Sanctification, like reconciliation and justification, is the act of God.[18] Man is never the one who sanctifies but the one who is sanctified. The man who once belonged to the world, who was sold under the power of sin, has by the act of God's grace been made a "man of God." This is Paul's primary emphasis in his use of the word "sanctified."

4. Adoption

What happened in justification, Paul sometimes describes as adoption.[19] This word is found only five times in the New Testament, all of them in Paul (Rom. 8:15,23; 9:4; Gal. 4:5; Eph. 1:5). It is a legal term denoting the bestowal of the privileges of sonship on one who is not naturally a member of the family.[20] Paul uses it in this sense three times (Rom. 8:15; Gal. 4:5–6). The result of adoption is that we are "sons of God" (Gal. 4:6) and have received the Holy Spirit which enables us to cry, "Abba! Father!" (Gal. 4:6; Rom. 8:14).

Paul's use of the word does two things. First, it describes with vivid reality the Christian's new status as a son of God. Second, it suggests that our sonship is secondary and derived in contrast to the "essential and inherent sonship of Christ." [21] God in his grace, through the death of Christ, has "restored to our orphan spirits their Father and to the Father His lost children." [22] We who once were "outsiders" are now members of the family of God.

5. In Christ—Union with Christ

Placing this idea last in this section is not meant to imply that it was unimportant to Paul. Rather, it is one of Paul's favorite terms for the initial experience of salvation and for the continuing life of the Christian.[23] Stewart calls it "the heart of Paul's religion." Paul's most characteristic sentences are those describing his "intense intimacy with Christ." [24] The evidence confirms this opinion. The expression is found over one hundred times in Paul's letters (eleven in Romans; eleven in 1 Cor.; ten in 2 Cor.; six in Gal.).

What did Paul mean by this expression? An exact definition is impossible; the expression is highly figurative and enigmatic. Some have called it mystical. The expression undoubtedly speaks of an intimate, dynamic, constant union with Christ.[25] Paul could say that for him to live was for Christ to live in the world (Phil. 1:21). His life was so dominated by

Christ and identified with him that Paul no longer lived, but Christ lived in him (Gal. 2:20).[26] One writer has said that Paul thought of himself as the alter ego of Christ. He insists that this points to Paul's mental instability.[27] Paul thought of it as the norm of Christian life.

He did not think of being "in Christ" as the loss of his own identity. We are saved "in Christ," not "lost" in him. Whatever union with Christ does, it enables a man to become himself, the true self with all the individuality for which God created him." [28] In the sense of lost identity, Paul was not a mystic.[29] His piety was not the kind that seeks emotion and ecstasy for their own sake, nor did it dissolve into speculation and lack of moral rectitude.[30]

But if we define mysticism as communion with God, an immediate awareness of God, a direct and intimate consciousness of God's presence,[31] Paul was a mystic.[32] For him, "to be in Christ means that Christ is within the Christian, addressing, guiding, comforting, rebuking, forgiving, strengthening him for life's tasks." [33] To be in Christ is to have a relation with him like that of the branches to the grapevine (John 15:1), like that of a building to its foundation (1 Cor. 3:10–11), like that of the members of the body to its head (Rom. 12:4–8; 1 Cor. 12:12–26), and like that of husbands and wives to each other (Eph. 5:22–23).

Analogies may enlighten; they cannot explain. The only explanation of Paul's meaning is Christian experience. There can be no doubt that union with Christ dominates Paul's thinking. It was, to him, a treasure beyond price.[34] Every major doctrine is connected with the formula. In Christ we are justified (Rom. 8:1–2); in Christ we are made new creatures (2 Cor. 5:17); in Christ we are made children of God (Gal. 3:26).[35] In Christ we are saints (Phil. 1:1; 4:21), sanctified (1 Cor. 1:2), have access to the Father (Eph. 3:12), and need not fear condemnation (Rom. 8:1).[36] Being in him assures us of the final resurrection (1 Thess. 4:16; 1 Cor. 15:22). Being in Christ brings power, strength, joy, gladness, and confidence to the Christian (Phil. 4:13; Gal. 5:10).

Salvation meant a new and vital relationship with God. Paul could describe this new relationship by a variety of terms—justification, reconciliation, sanctification, adoption, or being "in Christ." He meant essentially the same thing by each term. The old effort to divide Paul's thought into two parts—the legal and the vital—is lost effort. Paul had no concept of salvation which was purely legal; every concept denoted a vital relationship with God. Nor did he have any concept that was purely "mystical" and "otherworldly"; every concept pointed to a responsible relationship to be lived out in this world of time and space.

II. A New Self

If we avoid the danger of making each of Paul's words refer to only one aspect of salvation rather than the whole, we may profitably distinguish between the words which speak of salvation as fellowship with God and those which emphasize the creation of a new self. For Paul, these constituted a single whole. But we, as he, must look at the whole from various viewpoints in order to appreciate the full meaning of salvation.

Sin not only destroys fellowship with God; it also destroys the humanity of man. "For there is no distinction; since all have sinned and fall short of the glory of God" (Rom. 3:22–23). An increasing number of scholars interpret "glory of God" in this verse to mean the "glory" God meant man to have. Whether we had sinned or not, no man would ever measure up to the glory that belongs only to God. The emphasis of the verse is that sin is a destructive, corrupting power in human life. Because of sin, man has lost his integrity, his identity, and his true selfhood. He has become substandard, subhuman. The "image of God" in him has been distorted. He has lost his ability for loving fellowship with God and man. He is hounded by anxiety and fear, beset by enemies within and without.

Paul uses a number of expressions to describe the condition of man in sin. First, he is deceived; his life is a delusion. He seeks to satisfy his soul, but what he seeks no more satisfies his need than salt water will slake a man's thirst. Paul says, "We ourselves were once foolish, disobedient, led astray" (Titus 3:3). He reminds the Corinthians that "when you [did not know God], you were led astray to dumb idols" (1 Cor. 12:2).

Second, man in sin is enslaved. He has thrown off the "yoke of God" and thinks himself free. His imagined freedom is a delusion. He is "helpless" (Rom. 5:6) and "in bondage to beings that by nature are no gods" (Gal. 4:8).

Third, he is corrupted. Because of his rebellion, God has delivered him up to "impurity" (Rom. 1:24), "dishonorable passions" (Rom. 1:26), and "a base mind and improper conduct" (Rom. 1:28).

Fourth, he is dead "in trespasses and sins" (Eph. 2:1, 5). Sin has slain him (Rom. 7:9). The processes of death already sweep over his life. He is separated from good, love, and God.

Now, salvation reverses and more than reverses this process of human deterioration. Faith in Christ and the active power of God in man's life creates a new life. There are several words and expressions which Paul uses in his letters to churches to stress this fact.

1. Life

Opposite Paul's idea that sin is death is his idea that salvation is life. "Paul's most positive word for personal salvation is *life*." [37] The believer "shall live" (Rom. 1:17); he shall "reign in life" (Rom. 5:17); he walks in "newness of life" (Rom. 6:4). The obedience of Christ means "life for all men" (Rom. 5:18). the "law of the Spirit of life" has set man free from the "law of sin and death" (Rom. 8:1–2). The conversion of the Jews will lead to "*life* from the dead" (Rom. 11:15). To those who are saved, the gospel ministry is "a fragrance from *life to life*" (2 Cor. 2:16). Christ "died for us so that whether we wake or sleep we might *live* with him" (1 Thess. 5:10). These passages show how important the concept of life is to Paul's doctrine of salvation. We are tempted to say that Paul was using these words metaphorically, that the sinner is not really dead and that the Christian was alive before he was saved. But to Paul, the death of the sinner and the life of the believer were realities. The life that man was intended to have comes only when he is united with Christ Jesus.

2. New Creation

The idea of salvation as life is enriched by those expressions in Paul's letters which speak of it as *creation*. This is not a common expression in Paul, but when he does use it, he introduces it without explanation as if it were a well-known concept.

"For neither circumcision counts for anything, nor uncircumcision, but a *new creation*" (Gal. 6:15). "Therefore, if any one is in Christ, he is a *new creation;* the old has passed away, behold, the new has come" (2 Cor. 5:17). "The letter kills; the spirit *makes alive*" (2 Cor. 3:6). Baptism is the symbol of the experience of dying to our old self and arising to a new life (Rom. 6:1–2). The concept of salvation as a new creation is contained in Paul's figure of Christ as the last Adam. "The last Adam became a *life-giving* spirit" (1 Cor. 15:45, italics mine).

By speaking of salvation as creation, Paul is emphasizing two facts. One, salvation is a creation out of nothing; it is not just a reshaping of the old man. Two, salvation brings the life to man that God intended him to have.

3. Salvation

The New Testament uses salvation for the whole experience of becoming a Christian. In doing this, we have followed the pattern of the New Testament. Paul shares this word with the other New Testament writers, being responsible for less than half of its uses. The verb "to save" and the noun "salvation" occur forty-seven times in Paul's writings. Two moments of salvation are expressed by the term: (1) the initial experience of the Christian—i.e., his conversion and (2) the final experience of the Christian life—its consumation in heaven. The division is about half and half in Paul. Conner seems to be wrong in thinking that Paul used the word in a third sense to describe the process of growth in grace.[38]

Salvation includes two ideas which merge in the thought of Paul—healing and deliverance.[39] To be saved can mean to be healed of a disease; it is translated by "healed" or "made whole" in the miracle stories of the Gospels. When viewed from this point of view, sin is a spiritual disease from which man is delivered when he believes. To be saved can also mean to be delivered: "It is deliverance from the blight and curse of sin."[40] In Paul, the two ideas merge and make salvation into a positive term. It is not simply deliverance from danger and death, not simply a negative matter. It is bringing the believer into the fulness of life and blessing. It is the "realization of all man's spiritual potentialities in communion with God."[41]

The word suggests that when a man yields his total allegiance unto God in Christ, salvation "brings integrity to man's heart and unity of direction to his multifarious interests."[42] Salvation means fulfillment of life in *this world.* Fulfillment is not a static, but a dynamic, conception. Salvation is thus "actualizing in man's life what he (God) intends man's life to be."[43]

The believer finds a new self-identity in Christ. He is a child of God (Rom. 1:1). Once he was a slave to sin; now he is a slave to Christ (Rom. 1:1). But this new slavery is not slavish; paradoxically, it is freedom: "For freedom Christ has set us free" (Gal. 5:1). He once was helpless; now he has power over all things (1 Cor. 3:21-22). He was dead to God and good; now nothing can separate him from the love of God in Christ Jesus (Rom. 8:39). He once was like a rudderless ship, blown by every wind and wave; now he is a man of purpose with power to achieve that purpose (Phil. 4:13). In other words, the believer is for the first time in his life *a man,* a *true man,* the kind of man God created man to be.

III. A New Hope

Paul is so amazed, so astounded, so absorbed in the thought of what salvation means in the present that he does not dwell at length on what it means in the future. His main concern was to convince his readers that "God's unspeakable gift of grace was a realized fact." [44] Yet the idea of hope is woven into the fabric of this theology. It was one of the elements in his eternal triad—faith, hope, and love—which would abide when the need for partial knowledge and clouded speech were over. Not only here (1 Cor. 13), but in all of Paul's instruction, hope is an inseparable companion of love. "Eschatology cannot be written out of Paul's theology." [45]

Paul did not have an eschatological system. His statements on the subject are diverse and dispersed. For that reason it is impossible for us to turn his statements into a system.[46]

1. The Nature of Paul's "Hope"

Hope is an English word which varies in meaning with regard to degree of expectation of the thing hoped for. It always denotes an expectation of the future, but the expectation can be ephemeral or confident. For the Judaizer, hope had little expectation, no assurance. In Paul's vocabulary, hope is always confident assurance. The future consumation of salvation was not in doubt. The "not yet" was guaranteed by the "already." It is just when he speaks of the future that he becomes emphatic and dogmatic. "*I am sure* that he who began a good work in you will bring it to completion at the day of Jesus Christ" (Phil. 1:6, italics mine). "We *know* that if this earthly tent we live in is destroyed, we have a building from God, a house not made with hands, eternal in the heavens" (2 Cor. 5:1, italics mine). He uses the impersonal verb "must" to speak of the resurrection from the dead (1 Cor. 15:53). The verb means, "it is necessary in God's purpose" that this be so. He says, "we *shall* also bear the image of the man of heaven" (1 Cor. 15:49, italics mine).

However, Paul did not presume on the grace of God. While he was sure, he warned his readers on more than one occasion that their future depended on their faithfulness and watchfulness. "Therefore," he said, "let any one who thinks that he stands take heed lest he fall" (1 Cor. 10:12). To the Gentile Christians whose chance of salvation came because of the Jews' disbelief, he said: "Be not highminded, but fear: For if God spared not the natural branches, take heed lest he also spare not thee" (Rom. 11:20–21, KJV). Paul certainly did not subscribe to the notion that one could remain a Christian without remaining a Christian. In some verses, he speaks as if the matter were already settled; in other verses, he speaks as it were still hanging in the balance. Though paradoxical, these are not contradictory. Paul believed that a Christian must remain true to God if he were to be finally saved; he also believed that a believer *could* and *would* remain true. His assurance was not based on a mechanical *preservation of the saints* but on a dynamic *perseverance of the saints.*

2. The Bases of Hope

Why could Paul be so sure of the future consummation of salvation? There are several reasons. Hope does not exist of itself and its emotion; it is based on what "God has done and will do for believers . . . beyond man's potentialities." [47]

(1) *He believed in the dynamic meaning of initial salvation.* What happened to the believer when he yielded himself to the lordship of Christ was so transcendent that Paul never doubted that the true believer would continue in his faith. To Paul, conversion was a "disease" from which no man could recover; it was irreversible. This is why he could believe that the issue was still hanging in the balance and yet that it was already settled. "Having been justified by faith let us continue to live at peace with God through our Lord Jesus Christ, through whom also we have had access into this grace in which we took our stand and still stand" (Rom. 5:1–2, literal translation of the oldest text).

See how Paul thinks of the conversion experience. The believer has already been justified; the sentence of "no condemnation" has been pronounced upon him. This sentence is an anticipation of the future judgment; because of it the Christian can "face the future with confidence and courage." [48] The believer has had entree into the grace of God; he took his stand there and still stands there and will stand there (note: the Greek perfect tense). Therefore, he can eagerly await the hope—final righteousness (Gal. 5:5). He must stand; he will stand. His final salvation is guaranteed by the quality of his initial salvation.

All that we have said about salvation creating a new and lasting relation with God and a new self is relevant here. It need not be repeated; it should not be forgotten.

(2) *The possession of the Holy Spirit guarantees final salvation.* Paul declared, "Hope does not disappoint us, because God's love has been poured into our hearts through the Holy Spirit which has been given to us" (Rom. 5:5). Hope is not an illusion. All believers have received the "spirit of sonship" that prevents their falling back "into fear" and enables them to call God "Father" and guarantees that they are "heirs of God" and "fellow heirs with Christ" (Rom. 8:14–17).

Paul used a number of metaphors to stress this point. Using the metaphor of the full harvest which is guaranteed by the first fruits, he calls the Holy Spirit the "first fruits," that is, the "foretaste," of heaven (Rom. 8:23). Using the analogy of the marketplace, he speaks of the Holy Spirit as the "earnest money," that is, the "down payment," on our final inheritance (2 Cor. 1:22; 5:10). Using the law of contracts, he speaks of the Holy Spirit as the "seal" by which God establishes us in Christ (1 Cor. 1:21–22).[49] Basic to the understanding of Romans 8:18–30 is the fact that the possession of the Spirit "is described here as the basis of hope."[50]

(3) *The purpose of God formed the third basis* for Paul's assurance. "For whom he foreknew he also predestined to be conformed to the image of his Son, in order that he might be the firstborn among many brethern. And those whom he predestined he also called; and those whom he called he also justified; and those whom he justified he also glorified" (Rom. 8:29–30). Using the dramatic past tense, Paul speaks of the whole sweep of salvation as if it had already occurred. Foreknowledge, predestination, calling, justification, and glorification are linked in an unbreakable chain. It reaches from eternity to eternity. Since salvation in its consummation as well as in its beginning is rooted in the eternal purpose of God, Paul could speak of it as having already happened.

The same thought is found in 1 Corinthians 15:20–28. In this passage, Paul argues for the resurrection of the believer as a necessary link in the chain by which God's sovereignty over all things will be established. The chain of events is the resurrection of Christ—the reign of Christ until all enemies are subdued—the resurrection of believers by which death, the final enemy, is overcome—the deliverance of all things to God. Paul viewed this series of events as an unbreakable chain. If God's final sovereignty were to be established, no element in it could fail. The believer's final resurrection and victory over death and sin were thus guaranteed.[51] No power on earth, in heaven, or below earth can condemn God's elect. "It is God who justifies" (Rom. 8:33).

(4) *The constant care of God for his children* in their struggles against Satan and sin guarantees the final salvation of the believer. The quality of the conversion experience guarantees, not that the believer will not occasionally fall into sin, but that he will not remain in it. He may fall, but he will try to get up. The constant care of God guarantees that when he tries to get up, he *can.*

Coupled with the warning, "Let any one who thinks he stands take heed lest he fall" (1 Cor. 10:12) is the promise: "God is faithful, and he will not let you be tempted beyond your strength, but with the temptation will also provide the way of escape, that you may be able to endure it (1 Cor. 10:13). Paul was sure that no believer could stand in his own strength; he was equally sure that strength from God would always be available to him.

How could he be sure? Because of what God had already done. He had already "reconciled" us to himself "by the death of his Son" (Rom. 5:10). Because of God's unspeakable gift in the past, we can now, not as enemies, but as sons, be sure that we "shall be saved by his life" (Rom. 5:10). In Paul's victory song (Rom. 8:31–39) he challenges all the forces of death and hell to battle, confident of the believer's victory. "If God is for us, who is against us?" We can be sure that "God is for us" because "he spared not his own Son but gave him up for us all." What can this mean but that "he will give us all things with him"? (v. 32). Nothing will ever be able to separate us from the love of God in Christ Jesus (v. 39). Paul confidently shouts that we are "super-conquerers" through him that loved us (v. 37). The list of experiences which might separate (v. 35) and the forces that might conquer us (v. 38–39) is well nigh exhaustive. Paul challenges them all, sure that in the love of God he will be, as he had often been, victorious. Can we be any less sure?

3. The Content of Paul's Hope

Having discussed this previously, we will not need to discuss it again at length. Briefly, hope looked for the return of Jesus from heaven to receive his own (1 Thess. 1:9–10; 4:13–18). It expected the bodily resurrection, which was not a mere resuscitation but a complete transformation of life (Phil. 3:20–21; 1 Cor. 15:53–57). In a word, hope looked for the consummation of salvation (Rom. 13:11), the addition of the "not yet" to the "already." The Christian name for this expectation is heaven, a life of perfect bliss in the presence of God with no fear that it will ever be disturbed or destroyed.

4. The Meaning of Hope for the Present

One is convinced, after reading Paul's letters, that he did not speak of hope merely in joyful anticipation of the future but as a way to inspire the believer for the present. The present sufferings were unworthy of comparison with the coming glory (Rom. 8:18). No anxiety or faintheartedness or indolence could live in the same heart with assured hope (Phil. 4:4–9).[52] Grief for departed loved ones was eased by the hope of their resurrection and ours (Phil. 4:13). Christian living in the world of darkness is demanded by hope (Rom. 3:12). Steadfastness in "the work of the Lord" is possible because of the assurance that "in the Lord your labor is not in vain" (1 Cor. 15:58). Hope not only brightens the future; it also casts its glory before it over the scenes of the present. Victory is coming; we may anticipate it with assurance even in the midst of the darkest battle.

IV. A New Relation to Others

It might be argued that the believer's new relation to others is a result of, rather than an element in, salvation. Two things lead me to treat it as an element in salvation. One, the fundamental divisive factor in human relations is sin. Since salvation is a reversal of sin, it must introduce a new relation to others. Two, our relationship to others is so inextricably bound up with our relationship with God that they cannot be separated. Of course, in both directions, a distinction, but not a separation, can be made between the fundamental attitude which salvation creates and the living out of that attitude in life. The creation of the attitude is an element in salvation.

Our world is a divided world, and this division is primarily rooted in human sin. All divisions which cannot be overcome by material means have their source in sin. Sin causes one to look on his fellowmen as enemies, as a means to his own ends; it leads man to seek his own profit at the expense of others. Sin breeds selfishness, bias, prejudice, hatred, and apathy toward others which are fundamental factors in division.

Paul sees a creative relationship between reconciliation to God and reconciliation to man. In Galatians 3:26-28, he states that through our union with Christ Jesus, we have become sons of God through faith (v. 26). In being baptized with reference to Christ, we have "put on Christ" (v. 27). One possible interpretation of the metaphor, "put on Christ," is that we have undertaken to play the role of Christ. Though the expression was most commonly used to speak of people putting on clothing, "put on" was also used for an actor who put on a mask and assumed a new role on the stage. "In Christ," there is "neither Jew nor Greek"—racial barriers have been transcended. There is neither "slave nor free"—cultural barriers have been overcome. There is "neither male nor female"—natural barriers have been broken down. The reason: all have become "one in Christ Jesus" (v. 28).

A like statement is found in Colossians 3:11. Here, the racial barriers between "Greek and Jews," the religious barriers between the "circumcised and uncircumcised," and the cultural barriers between "barbarian,

Scythian, slave [and] free man" have been eliminated. Christ has become all things and dwells in union with all men. A new center of gravity, a new link between men has been established.

Salvation creates a basis for a new relationship with men. By overcoming the self and enthroning Christ, salvation opens the way for a relationship of mutual love and concern between men. Living out that relationship is not easy; without the creative power of salvation, it is impossible. Christ bridges the chasms between men. What separates men still remains, but it has been overcome in Christ.

NOTES

1. Käsemann, *Perspectives*, p. 70.   2. Stewart, *A Man in Christ*, p. 250.
3. Bultmann, *Theology*, I, pp. 274, 279.
4. G. B. Stevens, *New Testament Theology* (New York: Scribner's, 1908), p. 283.
5. W. Lowrie, "About Justification by Faith Alone," *Journal of Religion*, Oct., 1952, p. 235.
6. Vincent Taylor, *Forgiveness and Reconciliation* (London: Macmillan, 1946), p. 57.
7. Käsemann, *New Testament Questions*, p. 174.
8. Cf. Stewart, *A Man in Christ*, p. 248.
9. Conner, *Faith*, p. 335.   10. *Ibid.*, p. 336.
11. *Ibid.*, p. 338; Bultmann, *op. cit.*, p. 286.
12. E. C. Blackman, "Reconciliation, Reconcile," IDB 4, pp. 16–17; cf. Bultmann, *op. cit.*, p. 286.
13. *A Man in Christ*, pp. 209–211.
14. Conner, *Faith*, p. 337; Bultmann, *op. cit.*, p. 286.
15. Stewart, *op. cit.*, p. 257.
16. C. T. Craig, "Paradox of Holiness," *Interpretation*, Apr., 1952, p. 151.
17. Conner, *op. cit.*, p. 341.   18. Craig, *op. cit.*, p. 160.
19. Stewart, *op. cit.*, p. 254.   20. Conner, *op. cit.*, p. 339.
21. C. F. D. Moule, "Adoption," IDB 1, p. 43.
22. McLeod Campbell, *The Nature of the Atonement*, p. 147.
23. Conner, *Faith*, p. 346; cf. Barclay, *Mind of St. Paul*, p. 121.
24. *A Man in Christ*, p. 147.
25. Davies, *Paul and Rabbinic Judaism*, p. 87.
26. Conner, *Faith*, p. 346.
27. Hugh J. Schonfield, *The Jew of Tarsus* (New York: Macmillan, 1947), p. 99–101.
28. James Denney, *Reconciliation*, p. 307.
29. Stewart, *op. cit.*, p. 166.   30. *Ibid.*, pp. 160–161.
31. Alfred Wikenhauser, *Pauline Mysticism* (New York: Herder and Herder, 1960), p. 14.
32. Georgia Harkness, *Mysticism* (Nashville: Abingdon Press, 1973), p. 20.
33. *Ibid.*, p. 49.   34. Wikenhauser, *op. cit.*, p. 27.
35. Conner, *Faith*, p. 346; cf. Fritz Neugebaur, *In Christus* (Göttingen: Vandenhoeck & Ruprecht, 1961).
36. Wikenhauser, *op. cit.*, p. 26.
37. W. R. Nelson, "Pauline Anthropology," *Interpretation*, Jan., 1960, p. 19.
38. Conner, *Faith*, p. 335.   39. Clasper, *New Life in Christ*, pp. 14–15.
40. Conner, *op. cit.*, p. 334.   41. *Ibid.*
42. Paul S. Minear, "The Hope of Salvation," *Interpretation*, July, 1949, p. 262.
43. Paul Lehmann, "Deliverance and Fulfillment," *Interpretation*, October, 1951, p. 390.
44. Stewart, *A Man in Christ*, p. 262.   45. Bornkamm, *Paul*, p. 219.
46. *Ibid.*, p. 224.   47. *Ibid.*, p. 223.
48. Stewart, *A Man in Christ*, p. 269.   49. *Ibid.*, p. 263.
50. Käsemann, *An Die Römer*, p. 220.   51. Bornkamm, *Paul*, p. 225.
52. *Ibid.*, p. 226.

8
LIVING IN CHRIST

Paul complained that he had been "slanderously" accused of preaching: "Do evil that good may come" (Rom. 3:8). The Judaizers thought Paul's Achilles tendon was at the point of morality. They could not understand how the gospel, as Paul preached it, could avoid leading to sin. As they preached it, keeping the law followed faith as a necessary condition of being saved. Paul denied their accusations. He recoiled in horror to the idea that "we . . . continue in sin that grace may abound" (Rom. 6:1). To him it was unthinkable.

Paul believed salvation demanded a life of righteousness and guaranteed it. Scholars have often pointed out the paradox in Paul's letters between the indicative and imperative. Many statements seem inconsistent or self-contradictory.[1] There are statements that the justified one is free from sin; alongside them are other statements which exhort him to fight against sin.[2] He joins the absolute and the relative.[3] This paradox has often led men to think Paul excused sin in the Christian life. But this is far from the truth.

He thought of sin as a self-contradiction, a failure to be what you are. The Christian life, Paul thought, was based upon and derived from the fact of a new creation.[4] Christian living was simply bringing to full expression in one's experience, that is, working out to its completion, the salvation which God had wrought within the heart (Phil. 2:12-13). The whole meaning of the Christian life for Paul could be summarized in the imperative: *be what you are.* Over and over again, Paul joins in the closest possible relationship the statements of reality and the commands to performance. "If [rather, since] we live by the Spirit, let us also walk by the Spirit" (Gal. 5:25). "Since we are justified . . . let us rejoice in our sufferings" (Rom. 5:1-3, my translation of the best text). "So you also must consider yourselves dead to sin and alive to God in Christ Jesus. Let not sin therefore reign in your mortal bodies, to make you obey their passions" (Rom. 6:11-12). To Paul, there was no contradiction in this. The imperative did not limit the certainty of the indicative; the indicative did not weaken the imperative.[5] The indicative did not mean that the Christian need no longer struggle against *sins;* it meant that he had been freed from the dominion of *sin.*

What did *being yourself* mean to Paul? Among other things, it meant living like Christ, living in the church, and walking in the Spirit.

I. Living Like Christ

"The goal of the new existence of the saved man is to be transformed into the likeness of Christ."[6] Again and again, Paul emphasizes this goal. The "good" which God works for through the experiences of life (Rom. 8:28) is that we might be conformed to the "image of his Son" (Rom. 8:29). This transformation of character will be complete only when Christ comes (Phil. 3:21), but its beginning is located in this life on earth.[7] Paul would agree with C. S. Lewis: "Every Christian is to become a little Christ. The whole purpose of becoming a Christian is simply that, nothing else."[8]

Conformity to the image of Christ was Paul's personal goal. His ministry had as its aim: "that the life of Jesus may be manifested in our mortal flesh" (2 Cor. 4:11). He could be so bold as to say "Christ . . . lives in me" (Gal. 2:20) and "For me to live is Christ" (Phil. 1:21). One aim of his renunciation of his fleshly advantages was that "I may know him and the power of his resurrection, and may share his sufferings, becoming like him in his death" (Phil. 3:10). He could admonish his converts: "Be imitators of me," but only to the extent that "I am of Christ" (1 Cor. 11:1).

Not only for himself, but for his converts, the goal was to be like Christ. He did not consider himself a spiritual genius; he thought of likeness to Christ as a challenge to every believer.[9] To his Galatian converts, he could write: "My little children, with whom I am again in travail until Christ be formed in you!" (Gal. 4:19). "Until Christ be formed in you" suggests that they are now the embryo developing toward its ultimate goal. The fruition of their Christian experience will come only when they are like Christ.[10] Paul often pointed to the personal example of Jesus. Jesus did not "please himself" (Rom. 15:3); the Christian is not to "please himself" (v. 1) but to "please his neighbor for his good, to edify him" (v. 2). In other words, the Christian is to conform to the pattern of Christ. Humility and concern for each other is following the example of Christ in his incarnation and death on Calvary (Phil. 2:1-9). "The meekness and gentleness of Christ" could become the basis

LIVING IN CHRIST   **121**

for Paul's exhortation to faithfulness (2 Cor. 10:1). To imitate Christ is part and parcel of Paul's ethic.[11]

What did the imitation of Christ mean for Paul? Many things. The important ones can be summarized under four headings: responsible freedom, love, righteousness, and participation in God's work.

1. A Life of Responsible Freedom

"Freedom" was Paul's war cry in his fight against the Judaizers. He accused the Judaizers of being "false brethren" who had sneaked in "to spy out our freedom which we have in Christ Jesus, that they might bring us into bondage" (Gal. 2:4). He admonished his converts: "For freedom Christ has set us free; stand fast therefore, and do not submit again to a yoke of slavery" (Gal. 5:1). "Where the Spirit of the Lord is, there is freedom," Paul shouted (2 Cor. 3:17).

For Paul, freedom meant freedom from the law. While Paul still observed the ethical demands of the law, much of the law had become invalid for his Christian life. Paul practiced a discerning discrimination in his relationship with others. To the Jew he became as a Jew; though he did not consider himself under the law. To the Gentile he became "as one outside the law" (1 Cor. 9:20–21). He felt that the believer not only could but should differentiate between the valid and nonvalid requirements of the law.[12] He must "approve what is excellent" (Phil. 1:10)—that is, distinguish between the important and unimportant. He must "prove what is the will of God, what is good and acceptable and perfect" (Rom. 12:2). He could cry out, "All things are lawful for me" (1 Cor. 6:12).

The believer was also set free from the tyranny of sin. He was to "consider" himself "dead to sin and alive to God in Christ Jesus" (Rom. 6:11). "Slavery to sin" was a condition of the past that did not pertain to the present (Rom. 6:17). The Christian had "been set free from sin" (Rom. 6:18,22). The change in the believer's situation is: "For sin will have no dominion over you, since you are not under law but under grace" (Rom. 6:14). In Paul's mind, slavery to sin was slavery to the law, and slavery to the law was slavery to sin. God's grace in Christ had set the believer free.

I have tried to state Paul's freedom stand as baldly as possible so that the true radicalness of it can be seen. It is little wonder that his enemies accused Paul of preaching grace as an excuse for sin, nay, an encouragement to sin. From their standpoint, only the authority of an external regulation could discourage sin. If the law did not have authority over the believer, the way was open to unrestricted sinfulness.

This was to misunderstand Paul. Paul rejected freedom that released a man from all obligations and gave free reign to subjective caprice.[13] Paradoxically, *freedom was gained through slavery.* "Having been set free from sin you have become slaves of righteousness" (Rom. 6:18). "You have died to the law . . . so that you may belong to another," (Rom. 7:4).

Being set free then was not so much being *set free from* but *being set free for.* The alternative was not "to serve sin" versus "to do what I desire," but "to serve sin" versus "to serve the Lord (or righteousness)" (Rom. 6:16).[14] Freedom did not mean freedom from all restraint but freedom from the tyranny of futile desires.[15] In Paul, there is no irresponsible freedom, no freedom to sin.[16] Paul could describe himself as "not being myself under the law," but he hurried to add, "not being without law toward God but under the law of Christ" (1 Cor. 9:20–21).

Freedom did not destroy responsibility. The law, in so far as it was "good" and "holy" (Rom. 7:12) still commanded the Christian. It was the law, not its demands which was put to an end by the coming of Christ.[17] Though Paul could agree with his Corinthian friends that "all things are lawful for me" (1 Cor. 6:12), he hastened to add, "but not all things are helpful . . . but I will not be enslaved by anything."

Outer restraint had been superseded by inner restraint of a Christian character. Paul's freedom was meant only for those who themselves were free from the world and its claims, who were not motivated by worldly and fleshly desires.[18] He saw himself and his converts as "debtors, not to the flesh, to live according to the flesh" (Rom. 8:12) but to "live according to the Spirit" (Rom. 8:5).

Paul recognized that this was not easy. He knew that living "according to the Spirit" involved one in a state of civil war. He saw "flesh," that is, the old unsaved man, as still resident in the believer's life, though discredited and conquered. This lower nature of the Christian was constantly striving against the Spirit of God "to prevent you from doing what you would" (Gal. 5:16–17). The Christian's new self, however, had the upper hand. He could be admonished: "Let not sin therefore reign in your mortal bodies, to make you obey their passions" (Rom. 6:12). The Christian life is a life of striving; the believer is always faced with various possibilities. Reduced to its essence, this means that I must choose between living for self or living to God or the Lord (2 Cor. 5:14–15).

Situation ethics? No. Paul's letters are filled with various vices to be avoided and various virtues to be cultivated. Legalism? No. Obedience is always a matter of gratitude to God, the obedience of a free man seeking the glory of God. Licentiousness? No. The believer is always faced with the obligation to do right and the responsibility of his own choices. Freedom? Yes. Freedom *from the tyranny of sin* and *freedom for the service of God.*

2. A Life of Love

God demands a life of love. Paul looked on love as faith manifesting itself in living.[19] The primary fruit of the Spirit in the believer's life is love (Gal. 5:22). "In Christ Jesus neither circumcision nor uncircumcision is of any avail, but faith working through love" (Gal. 5:6). "Owe no one anything, except to love one another; for he who loves his neighbor has fulfilled the law. . . . Love does no wrong to a neighbor; therefore love is the fulfilling of the law" (Rom. 13:8,10). It was God who taught the Thessalonians to "love one another" (1 Thess. 4:9–10). Paul admonished the Philippians to "abound more and more" in love (Phil. 1:9). Paul thought of love as the basic element of Christian living.

In the magnificent hymn to love (1 Cor. 13:1–13), Paul asserted that without love, the Christian preacher was in the same class as the pagan priest with his "noisy gong" and "clanging cymbal" (v. 1). The Christian prophet who knows all and has faith to move mountains is a zero, a nothing, without love (v. 2). The Christian martyr who gives his body to be burned gains nothing if he does not have love (v. 3). Love is greater than all conceivable "gifts of grace"; it gives meaning to them.[20]

In the second stanza, Paul turns to a positive characterization of what love means. In fifteen positive and negative statements, he outlines the qualities of love, qualities which many have often seen as a hidden description of Jesus himself (vv. 4–7). In each case, love is seen, not as an emotion, but as an active principle, manifesting itself in everyday relations.[21]

In the final stanza of the hymn (vv. 8–13), love's imperishability is set over against the "imperfection" of spiritual gifts, even those given by the Holy Spirit. "Tongues cease" (v. 8); "knowledge is imperfect"; "prophecy is imperfect" (v. 9). "The imperfect will pass away" (v. 10), but "faith, hope, love abide, these three; but the greatest of these is love" (v. 13).

Thus love becomes the primary Christian obligation. But the love Paul promoted is not the love of Hollywood. It is not erotic love, nor even the love that characterizes friendship. It is *agape. Agape* was a Greek word, seldom used in the Greek world because it was considered cold and unemotional. The New Testament writers, following the Greek translators of the Old Testament, adopted the word to speak of love in a special sense. As applied to God, it was love which was completely and unconditionally outgoing in creation, redemption, and providence.[22] As applied to man, it described love as devotion to God and unselfish concern for the welfare of others. Love began in the brotherhood of the saints and manifested itself in mutual helpfulness, encouragement, and restoration to Christian living. Love extended to outsiders and manifested itself in friendliness and concern for the conversion of all men.

3. *A Life of Righteousness*

Paul certainly did not encourage or excuse sin in the believer. Though the law of Moses was rejected as a way to life, its demands, in so far as they expressed the will of God, were still valid and binding.[23] The changed situation, wrought by God, did not consist of a new moral code but of the ability to perform "the just requirements of the law" (Rom. 8:4). Paul saw the demands of the law as "holy and just and good" (Rom. 7:12) and the law itself as "spiritual" (Rom. 7:14). He thought of the law as being an expression of God's own character and defining the kind of thing which God demands of those who seek to please him.

But Paul did not limit his demands to the law. He recognized, as Jesus had before him, that the law was inadequate; it could not define the life of righteousness. Paul therefore demanded that Christians go beyond the law in their Christian lives. "Since we have these promises, beloved, let us cleanse ourselves from every defilement of body and spirit, and make holiness perfect in the fear of God" (2 Cor. 7:1). He was not above borrowing from the pagan morality when he considered it good. So he said, "Finally, brethren, whatever is true, whatever is honorable, whatever is just, whatever is pure, whatever is lovely, whatever is gracious, if there is any excellence, if there is anything worthy of praise, think about these things" (Phil. 4:8). He admonished his converts to obey the civil authorities and pay their taxes. Since they are "ministers of God," resistance to them constituted resistance to God (Rom. 13:1–7).

Paul did not promote a legalistic spirit. The primary difference between his ethic and that of Judaism and the Stoics was motivation,[24] but that is a world of difference. Fulfillment of the law was not a meritorious achievement; it was a deed of freedom.[25] The moral actions of the new man in Christ has the "function of obedience" to God.[26] Paul also looked upon the moral life as a witness to outsiders. He urged the Thessalonians to live a life that would "command the respect of outsiders" (1 Thess. 4:11–12).

Paul expected the believer to grow in holiness. He spoke of the Christian as "being changed into his likeness from one degree of glory to another" (2 Cor. 3:18). He reprimanded the Corinthians for still being "fleshly" men (1 Cor. 3:3). He urged the Philippians to "abound more and more" in love (Phil. 1:9) and prayed for the Thessalonians: "May the Lord make you increase and abound in love to one another and to all men" (1 Thess. 3:12).

4. A Life of Service

One element of living in Christ is a life of service. Worship itself, in Paul's mind, was the yielding of our earthly lives to God for his use (Rom. 12:1; cf. 6:13). The Christian was to live no longer for himself but for the Christ who died for him (2 Cor. 5:15).

Paul's admonitions to be workers for the Lord are common in his letters. A sampling of them: abound "in the work of the Lord" (1 Cor. 15:58); count yourselves as "ambassadors for Christ" (2 Cor. 5:20); "bear fruit for God" (Rom. 7:4); do not "grow weary in well-doing" (Gal. 6:9); "never flag in zeal . . . serve the Lord" (Rom. 12:11). Strive "side by side for the faith of the gospel" (Phil. 1:27); "encourage one another and build one another up" (1 Thess. 5:11); "admonish the idle, encourage the fainthearted, help the weak, be patient with them all" (1 Thess. 5:14).

His greatest words of praise were for those who served in the work of Christ. His friends are described in various ways: "She has been a helper of many and of myself as well . . . my fellow workers in Christ . . . who has worked hard among you . . . our fellow worker in Christ . . . these workers in the Lord (Rom. 16:1–16).

He looked upon all Christians as having received gifts from the Lord and admonished them: "Having gifts that differ according to the grace given to us, let us use them: if prophecy, in proportion to our faith; if service, in our serving; he who teaches, in his teaching; he who exhorts, in his exhortation; he who contributes, in liberality; he who gives aid, with zeal; he who does acts of mercy, with cheerfulness" (Rom. 12:6–8).

Paul expected every believer to be a missionary; each member of the church was a functioning and working member. He demanded that every member should "bear his own burden" (Gal. 6:5, KJV) and insisted that the church grows only when "each part is working properly" (Eph. 4:16). There was no division between clergy and laity. All were priests and prophets. "There were no passive members." [27] "In the beginning of the Christian cause all were ministers." There were no observers, no mere supporters, no nominal members.[28]

II. Living in the Church

For Paul, there could be no such thing as an isolated Christian. Living in Christ meant living in the church, the assembly of the saints. Paul looked upon the churches as the primary channels of the gospel and essential to Christian life and service. All of his letters except Philemon are addressed directly or indirectly to churches. After listing a whole series of hardships and sufferings in the ministry of Christ (2 Cor. 11: 23–27), he adds: "And, apart from other things, there is the daily pressure upon me of my anxiety for all the churches" (v. 28).

Notice that he said "churches," not "Church." For Paul, a church was always a body of believers united to carry out the commands of Christ. In our day, many have tried to appropriate "church" to speak of the whole company of believers. Bornkamm insists that the church is "more and other" than the individual congregations. He looks upon the individual congregations as "simply giving historical form" to the whole church.[29] Bultmann is more cautious, but still in error. He says that *ekklēsia* is used sometimes for the "total Church" and sometimes for the "local congregation."[30] Opinions of the same order are common.

But they represent a misunderstanding of Paul. For Paul, the *ekklēsia* was the local congregation and nothing else.[31] It stood in direct relation to Christ and was not merely a "historical form" of something "more and other" than itself, unless you think of it as a historical form of Christ.

This follows from several considerations. (1) The Greek word commonly translated "church" (*ekklēsia*) was a common technical term for a "secular assembly of citizens."[32] It received its religious meaning in the Greek translation of the Old Testament where it was used "for the chosen people of Israel when assembled before God, as, for example, at Mount Sinai."[33] There is simply no linguistic evidence that the Greek word ever *was* used or *could* be used to designate people *not* assembled. (2) Wherever the context indicates the meaning of the word in the New Testament, it uniformly restricts it to the local congregation of God's people (i.e., by the use of the plural and of the singular with a place name). The context does not always (i.e., in about 17 of 114 uses in the New Testament) restrict the meaning to the local congregation. Yet, it never excludes this meaning. (3) Paul's concern was always for the local congregations; his ministry was always to and through them. He shows no evidence that he ever thought of the church as anything but the local congregation.

This does not mean that he did not have a theological conception of all believers as the "people of God" or "spiritual Israel." He did. He reminded the Corinthians that they shared the name "saints" "with all those who in every place call on the name of our Lord Jesus Christ, both their Lord and ours" (1 Cor. 1:2). He certainly believed that our common salvation made us all brothers in Christ, members of the household of God. *But he never called this reality a church.* Saints, heirs of Abraham, brothers? Yes. Church? No.[34] He felt that each church should be concerned about all the churches. Because of this, he was glad to promote an offering for the poor in Jerusalem among his Gentile congregations. Yet, he knew of nothing like our modern denominations.

You may ask: Why is this important? Since both realities existed, why be concerned if some scholars falsely assign the term "church" to the universal fellowship? Two reasons suggest that we follow Paul and restrict the use of "church" to the local congregation. (1) We seek to understand Paul; to give his words meanings which are foreign to him will lead to misunderstanding. (2) To admit the use of the term "church" to express the idea of a universal brotherhood of believers tends to take away from the local congregation its true dignity and meaning. Paul's most exalted terms for the church (i.e., "body of Christ" and "temple of the Holy Spirit") are often referred to the universal brotherhood rather than to the local congregation. Aside from the false exegesis that this causes, it leads some to think of the local congregations as something far less than what they were to Paul and should be to us.

Paul felt that each believer was a *member* of the assembly. By the use of "member" (which seems to have been original with Paul), he insists that the church is a spiritual organism rather than an earthly organization.[35] "Now you are the body of Christ and individually members of it" (1 Cor. 12:27). The "you" is the "church of God which is at Corinth" (1 Cor. 1:2). Membership in the body of Christ was based on union with Christ, but it implied a union with other members like that of the physical organism, the body. The oneness was created by the Holy Spirit and solemnized by baptism (1 Cor. 12:13).[36]

The union of members with one another carried weighty implications. It meant that there could be no jealousy on the part of the members who felt that they had lesser functions—all members were essential to the wholeness of the body. It meant that those who felt they had superior functions could not boast against the others—all members were essential to the wholeness of the body. It meant that the participation and function of each member of the body was necessary to the function of the whole (1 Cor. 12:14–25). These considerations outlaw discord in the body and demanded a unity which manifested itself in: "If one member suffers, all suffer [note: not should suffer, but do suffer] together; if one member is honored, all rejoice together" (1 Cor. 12:26).

In practice this meant that each member accepted unlimited responsibility for each other member. The church, in Paul's thinking, was to be a creative fellowship, a mutual improvement society, with each member helped and edified by the whole. Philippians 1:27 to 2:18 is one of the great "church" passages in Paul's letters. It begins: "Only let your manner of life be worthy of the gospel of Christ" (1:27). "Life" translates the Greek word from which we get our English word "politics." Thus, it refers not to the individual lives of the Christians, but to the corporate life of the church. Paul begged them to "live corporately," that is, as a congregation, in a way which was worthy of the gospel of Christ. What he meant by this is developed in the rest of the passage.

One thing it meant was "striving side by side for the faith of the gospel" (1:27). This was to be done with "one mind" (literally, one soul), that is, with a unified purpose. This striving was to be done with courage "not frightened . . . by your opponents" (1:28), with willingness to "suffer" for the gospel (1:29), and with an understanding that they were engaged in a spiritual warfare with the forces of evil even as Paul was (1:30). It was to be done without "grumbling or questioning" (2:14), with a character which demanded the respect of the pagan world (2:15). Such actions would assure Paul that his labor had not been in "vain" (2:16).

It is in the midst of this passage that Paul speaks of the unity of the church. Unity, he felt, was essential to the fulfillment of the church's mission in the world. Basing his appeal on the dynamic realities of the gospel (2:1), he says: "Complete my joy by being of the same mind, have the same love, being in full accord and of one mind" (2:2). Unity meant two things. (1) "Do nothing from selfishness or conceit, but in humility count others better than yourselves" (2:3). (2) "Let each of you look not only to his own interests, but also to the interests of others" (2:4). "Each of you" is plural in the Greek (an impossible form in English). It should have been translated: let each group among you be concerned about the interest of other groups, not just about its own."

This unity was not negative, that is, avoiding conflict; it was positive. The church ("your" is plural) was to "work out your own salvation" (2:12). "Work out" comes from a Greek word which means to "work out fully." Thus, the idea is not to "work for salvation" as if it were in doubt, but to "work out the salvation" which God had worked in, that is, to bring it to full expression in life. This was a mutual responsibility, each member must contribute to each other member. If any member failed, the church had failed. It was a serious task; they were to go about it "with fear and trembling." But it was a possible task: "For God is at work in [or among] you, both to will and to work for his good pleasure" (2:13).

Paul felt that church membership was essential to living and mission. By integration into the body of believers, each Christian found help in doing what he had to do and found opportunity to help others, thus becoming more like Christ himself. This note of mutual responsibility is one which Paul sounds again and again. His whole discussion of eating meat sacrificed to idols is dominated by the duty of mutual concern for each other's good (1 Cor. 8:1-13). "Love" not "knowledge" should determine a Christian's action in this area; "for love builds up" (8:1). The weaker brother's scruples should not be violated; the enlightened Christian must "take care lest this liberty of yours" lead the weaker Christian into sin (8:9). The individual believer must not act in such a way as to destroy his brother for whom Christ died (8:11). He must be willing to forego his own liberty of action to safeguard the life of his brother.

The same principle dominates Paul's discussion of the "weak" and the "strong" in Romans 14—15. Here, the scruples are wider in scope than eating meat offered to idols. The one who feels free to eat is not to "despise" the weaker brother; the weaker brother is not "to judge" the stronger (14:2-3). Each is to respect the sincere devotion of the other. The one who has scruples does what he does "in honor of the Lord"; that is, as obedience to Christ. The one without such scruples gives thanks to God; he also honors "the Lord"—he does what he does as an expression of his devotion to Christ (14:1-2). Neither is to pass judgment on the other: rather, "Let each of us please his neighbor for his good, to edify him" (15:2). Again the example of Christ is called into play: he "did not please himself" (15:3).

Again, the whole discussion of spiritual gifts (1 Cor. 12; 14) is dominated by the principle of mutual concern. "To each is given the manifestation of the Spirit for the common good" (12:7). This is the keynote of the whole passage which emphasizes that the variety of spiritual gifts are apportioned to by the Holy Spirit "to each one individually as he wills" (12:11). Then follows the discussion of the church as the body of Christ (12:14-27). After showing them the more excellent way of love (chap. 13), Paul turns to a comparison of "prophecy" and "speaking in tongues" (chap. 14). He values prophecy far more than speaking in tongues because "he who prophesies speaks to men for their upbuilding and encouragement and consolation" (14:3). Paul's conclusion is that the church services should be regulated by the rule: "Let all things be done for edification" (14:26).

But the church was more than a mutual improvement society, more than a corporate force in missions. It was a divine reality in the world.[37] As a corporate reality, it was "the church of God" (1 Cor. 1:2), "in God the Father and the Lord Jesus Christ" (1 Thess. 1:1), "sanctified in Christ Jesus," and "called to be saints" (1 Cor. 1:2). This was true in spite of the many imperfections which characterized the life of the churches. Aside from these expressions, Paul used, perhaps created, a number of striking metaphors to express the divine nature of each church.

He spoke of Christ as the foundation of the church. Using a building metaphor, he said: "you are God's . . . building" (1 Cor. 3:9). Then he added: "No other foundation can anyone lay than that which is laid, which is Jesus Christ" (1 Cor. 3:11).

What did he mean by this metaphor? It seems clear that he meant that the church was founded on the historical work and ministry of Jesus Christ. Remember that he had laid the foundation. How? By preaching Christ crucified and nothing else (1 Cor. 2:2). He said: "For I delivered to you as of first importance what I also received, that Christ died for our sins in accordance with the scriptures, that he was buried, that he was raised on the third day in accordance with the scriptures, and that he appeared (1 Cor. 15:3–5). Thus Paul connected the church with the historical Jesus. To depart from that foundation is to destroy the church, that is, to make it no longer the church.

Paul spoke of the church as *the body of Christ* about fifteen times. We have discussed this figure in defining the church as a "spiritual organism." What did it mean with reference to the church as a divine reality? It meant that the church is the reincarnation of Christ; it is the instrument of his continued action in the world. Paul did not think of Christ as an absentee owner of the church, but as a living part of it—its head.[38] His will, and that alone, is the goal of the church. His word, and that alone, is the authority of the church. By this figure, Paul expressed his belief in a dynamic, intimate, vital, living union between the church and its living Christ.

Again, Paul spoke of the church as *the temple of God.* To the Corinthians, he said: "You do know, do you not, that *a* temple of God you are, and the Spirit of God dwells in your midst? If any one destroys *the* temple of God, God will destroy this man. For *the* temple of God is holy, and you have this nature" (1 Cor. 3:16–17, my literal translation). The use of the article is important to the understanding of this passage. *The* temple refers to the inner sanctuary of the Old Testament times;[39] it is that reality which forms the basis of Paul's figure. The Corinthians are not *the* temple; the absence of the article means that they have the nature of being "temple of God." The English *a* is not exactly equivalent. The same thought is found in: "For God is at work among (or in) you, to enable you both to desire to do his good pleasure and to accomplish it" (Phil. 2:13, my paraphrase).

This was what the church was to Paul. He says little, if anything, about it as an establishment in the world, organized for orderly existence. No doubt, he assumed this; there is nothing inconsistent between organization and organism. Organization speaks of orderly procedures. Organism speaks of inner reality. Paul's emphasis was on the inner reality. He also emphasized the divine dimension of its existence, that it was founded on the work of the historical Jesus, ruled by the presence of its living Lord, and indwelt by God through the Holy Spirit.

III. Walking in the Spirit

"Walk in the Spirit and you will certainly not fulfill the desires of the flesh" (Gal. 5:16, my translation). The Revised Standard Version changes the second part of this sentence into an imperative; I think the indicative is demanded (cf. KJV). There is only one command, "Keep on walking in the Spirit." This is followed by the assured results of such a walk, "You will certainly not (double negative in Gk.) fulfill the desires of the flesh."

We may take this verse as a keynote in Paul's thought of what it meant to live in Christ; it meant walking in the Spirit. This, with living like Christ and living in the church, forms the great triad which encompasses the full meaning of living a Christian life. Paul does not have a formal doctrine of the Holy Spirit; his thoughts on the subject are diverse and dispersed. However, he does have four passages which more than any others speak of the nature and function of the Holy Spirit (cf. Rom. 8:2–27; 1 Cor. 2:1–13; 12:1–13; Gal. 5:15–23). I think it significant that these passages are located in the literature that deals most fully with the conflict with the Judaizers.

Where shall we begin? In the light of our modern climate, we need to make some preliminary statements. Much that is false is said on the subject; many have been "turned off" by the excesses of others. Paul relates the doctrine of the Holy Spirit to four major points in his theology—his doctrines of God, of Christ, of the church, and the Christian life. But his primary emphasis is on the work of the Spirit in the Christian life. Walking in the "Spirit" is what makes the Christian different from the natural man.[40] Let us detour briefly and then return to our central concern.

The Spirit is the Spirit of God, the way by which God in his fullness becomes present in human life. "God has sent the Spirit of his Son in our hearts" (Gal. 4:6). The Spirit is from God, proceeds from God,[41] and makes God's presence real in lives. Thus, "God's love has been poured into our hearts through the Holy Spirit which has been given to us" (Rom. 5:5).

There is one passage which almost seems to make the Spirit impersonal. "God has revealed to us through the Spirit. For the Spirit searches everything, even the depths of God. For what person knows a man's thoughts except the spirit of the man which is in him? So also no one comprehends the thoughts of God except the Spirit of God" (1 Cor. 2:10–11). The main thrust of the passage is the revealing function of the Spirit. God makes himself known to us through the Spirit; the Spirit is God's self-knowledge which he shares with us.[42] So far, so good. But the relation of the Spirit to God is compared to the relation of a man's spirit to himself and contrasted with "the spirit of the world" (v. 12). I suppose that we must assign this ambiguity to the poverty of language. Paul certainly did not think of the Spirit as an impersonal force or power, a mere emanation from God. He speaks of "the mind of the Spirit" (Rom. 8:27); he ascribes will to the Spirit in the passage: "All these are inspired by one and the same Spirit, who apportions to each one individually as he wills" (1 Cor. 12:11).[43] Any talk about the Spirit must be parabolic or figurative; there is no literal language for the Spirit. It is little wonder that Paul sometimes borders on identifying the Holy Spirit with God or Christ and sometimes borders on separating him from them. Two things are clear: (1) The Spirit is the Spirit of God. (2) The Spirit is personal.

The Spirit is the Spirit of Christ. Spirit enthusiasts tend to exalt the sovereign freedom of the Spirit and separate his work from Christ.[44] But Paul said: "Now the Lord is the Spirit, and where the Spirit of the Lord is, there is freedom" (2 Cor. 3:17). This verse illustrates the weakness of human language. In the first part, Paul seems to identify Christ and the Spirit; "The Lord is the Spirit." In the second part, he seems to separate them: "Where the Spirit of the Lord is." If we attempt to interpret this passage theologically, it makes nonsense. But if we interpret it experientially, it makes wonderful sense. From the point of view of Christian experience the presence of Christ and the presence of the Spirit cannot be distinguished; they amount to the same thing.[45] It is from this viewpoint that Paul speaks of the Spirit. Christ is present in the Spirit's presence. "The Spirit mediates to us the presence of Christ." [46] The Spirit is the true alter ego of Christ.[47] Because of this close association in experience, their names are often interchangeable.[48]

There can be no thought then of an experience with the Spirit "different from and other than" an experience with Christ. The idea that is prevalent in many circles that the reception of the Spirit is something subsequent to the reception of Christ, a kind of "second blessing" cannot be true. When one yields his allegiance to Christ, he receives the Holy Spirit. This is a part of what it means to be saved. "Any one who does not have the Spirit of Christ does not belong to him" (Rom. 8:9). "If Christ is in you" (Rom. 8:10) is obviously equal to "For all who are led by the Spirit of God are sons of God" (Rom. 8:14). The Holy Spirit is for all Christians, not for just a few.[49]

The Holy Spirit dwells in the churches. The church is a temple of God because "God's Spirit dwells in you" (1 Cor. 3:16). Without the indwelling Spirit, "there could be no such thing as the Christian church." [50] It is the Holy Spirit which gives the gifts to men which makes the work of the church possible (1 Cor. 12:7).

The Holy Spirit dwells in and helps all Christians. Now we are back to our central concern. The Christian life would be impossible without the "indwelling, stimulating, and directing" power of the Holy Spirit.[51] The Holy Spirit is the source of "all Christian life, its every gift, every virtue, every expression." [52] When we analyze the statements of Paul about the work of the Spirit in the Christian life, the list is striking.

The Spirit enables us to win the victory in our struggle for righteousness (Gal. 5:16–17; Rom. 8:4–5,12–13; 14:17). The Spirit enables us to worship God as we should (Phil. 3:3). The Spirit produces Christlike "fruits" in our lives (Gal. 5:22–23). "The fruits of the Spirit are nothing but the virtues of Christ." [53] The Spirit enables us to pray effectively (Rom. 8:26–27). The Spirit gives spiritual insight into the truths of God (2 Cor. 2:10–13).[54] The Spirit gives us power to preach effectively (1 Cor. 2:1–5). The Spirit gives the gifts for meaningful participation in the church (1 Cor. 12:1–11).

The Spirit is the "transforming and uplifting power of the Christian's whole inner life."[55] Often the Holy Spirit is connected with spectacular phenomena in such a way that people identify the Holy Spirit with such things. Certainly, we cannot write out of the New Testament the spectacular. However, the real tokens of his presence are "in the quiet, steady, normal life of faith."[56] A review of the things which Paul ascribes to the Spirit will show that most of these are not spectacular except in the sense that love, faith, and hope are spectacular.

Finally, there are degrees of the manifestation of the Spirit in Christian lives, and in the same life at different times. We speak of "possessing the Spirit." It would be better to speak of "the Spirit possessing us." When the Spirit controls our lives, when we "walk in the Spirit," the full measure of his presence can be realized. This is another way of saying that the degree of our devotion to Christ determines the degree of his power in our lives.

NOTES

1. Rall, *According to Paul*, p. 82.   2. Bultmann, *The Old and the New Man*, p. 7.
3. Rall, *op. cit.*, p. 83.
4. Richard Longenecker, *The Ministry and Message of Paul* (Grand Rapids: Zondervan, c. 1971), p. 100.
5. Günther Bornkamm, *Early Christian Experience*, p. 71.
6. Nelson, "Pauline Anthropology," p. 20.
7. F. W. Beare, *The Epistle to the Philippians* (New York: Harper, c. 1959), p. 35.
8. *Beyond Personality* (New York: Macmillan, 1945), p. 28.
9. Beare, *op. cit.*, p. 34.   10. Burton, *Galatians*, p. 248.
11. Davies, *Paul and Rabbinic Judaism*, p. 147.
12. Bultmann, *Theology*, I, p. 341.   13. *Ibid.*, p. 342.
14. Conzelmann, *Outline*, p. 279.
15. C. H. Dodd, *The Meaning of Paul for Today* (London: Swathmore Press, 1920), p. 137.
16. Conzelmann, *op. cit.*, p. 277.   17. *Ibid.*
18. Bultmann, *Theology*, I, p. 342.   19. *Ibid.*, p. 344.
20. Bornkamm, *Paul*, p. 217.   21. *Ibid.*, p. 218.
22. Cf. Nels F. S. Ferré, "The Given for Christian Theology," *Interpretation*, Jan., 1966, p. 29.
23. Bultmann, *Theology*, I, p. 341.   24. Wright and Fuller, *Acts*, pp. 309–310.
25. Bultmann, *Theology*, I, p. 344.   26. Bultmann, *The Old and the New Man*, p. 26.
27. Auguste Sabatier, *Religious Authority and the Religion of the Spirit* (New York: George H. Doran, 1904), pp. 71–72.
28. Elton Trueblood, *Alternative to Futility* (New York: Harper, 1948), p. 73.
29. *Paul*, p. 177.   30. *Theology*, I, p. 308.
31. D. E. Nineham ("The Case Against Pauline Authorship," *Studies in Ephesians*, ed. F. L. Cross, p. 32) uses the supposed use of *ekklesia* in Ephesians for the universal church as proof against Pauline authorship. I would agree that if this use could be established, it would be a telling argument against Pauline authorship. However, I believe that even Ephesians uses *ekklesia* only for the local congregation.
32. Bornkamm, *Paul*, p. 177; cf. Adolf Deissmann, *Light from the Ancient East* (New York: Harper, 4th ed., 1922), p. 2.
33. *Ibid.*

34. C. F. D. Moule, *Cambridge Lectures,* 1970–71; cf. Eduard Schweizer, "Unity and Diversity in the New Testament Teaching Regarding the Church," *Theology Today,* Jan., 1957, p. 47.
35. Conzelmann, *Outline,* p. 261.   36. Conner, *Faith,* p. 372.
37. R. M. Brown, *The Significance of the Church* (Philadelphia: Westminster Press, 1956), pp. 4–5.
38. W. M. Horton, "The Christian Community," *Interpretation,* Oct. 1950, p. 393.
39. Bornkamm, *Paul,* p. 180.   40. Wikenhauser, *Pauline Mysticism,* p. 54.
41. George S. Hendry, *The Holy Spirit in Christian Theology* (Philadelphia: Westminster Press, 1965), pp. 32–33.
42. *Ibid.,* p. 33.   43. Cf. Conner, *Faith,* p. 365.
44. Hendry, *op. cit.,* p. 68.   45. *Ibid.,* p. 25.
46. Conner, *Faith,* p. 364.   47. Hendry, *op. cit.,* p. 65.
48. Wikenhauser, *op. cit.,* p. 53.   49. Rall, *According to Paul,* p. 138.
50. W. T. Conner, *The Work of the Holy Spirit* (Nashville: Broadman Press, 1940), p. 131.
51. Conner, *Faith,* p. 367.   52. Rall, *op. cit.,* p. 138.
53. Friedrich Schleiermacher, *The Christian Faith* (Edinburgh: T. & T. Clark, 1948), p. 576.
54. Rall, *op. cit.,* p. 140.   55. Conner, *Faith,* p. 366.
56. Stewart, *A Man in Christ,* p. 308.

PART III
Paul: Opponent of the Gnosticizers

9
THE QUESTIONS

Because the Gnosticizers threatened to contaminate the gospel, Paul, the man of conflict,[1] opposed them just as he had the Judaizers. Two of his letters deal primarily with this conflict—Ephesians and Colossians. They were written to solve problems in the congregations to whom Paul felt obligated to minister.[2] A study of these letters leads to an understanding of the problems and the nature of Paul's answer to their challenge.

The doctrines preached by Paul's opponents have come, *in modern scholarship,* to be identified with gnosticism, a religious movement of the second century which sought to combine elements of pagan thought with the Christian gospel.[3] We must give more than passing notice to these doctrines, their origin and their development into gnostic systems.

I. Gnosticism

We cannot make a thorough study of gnosticism. Many books have been written about it.[4] It is necessary, however, to sketch the movement and identify the ideas which in pre-gnostic times were preparing the way for gnosticism.

1. Our Knowledge of Gnosticism

How much do we know about gnosticism? Much more now than fifty years ago. Prior to 1955 when W. C. Till published the Berlin Gnostic Codex, our knowledge consisted of statements about the Gnostics and quotations from their works by their opponents, particularly Irenaeus and Hippolytus.[5] One could suspect that our knowledge was not wholly trustworthy. Had these Christian Fathers presented a distorted picture of the movement in order to refute it? This did not turn out to be true. The Berlin Codex, the contents of which had been known for some time before its publication, confirmed the main outlines of the movement as presented by Irenaeus and Hippolytus.

Far more important, however, was the discovery of an ancient gnostic library at Nag Hammadi in central Egypt in 1945 and 1946. Published parts of this library contain more than forty gnostic documents in a thousand pages of text in good condition.[6] Consequently, scholars are much more sure of their knowledge of gnosticism than at any time in the past. Not all questions have been answered and all problems solved. Far from it. But the main lines of the gnostic movement are now clear.

2. The Roots of Gnosticism

Gnosticism was a syncretistic movement. It selected and combined elements from various sources. The ideas which it combined with Christian teachings in the second century were "in the air" in the first century. To call them gnostic ideas in the first century would be anachronistic; they became gnostic ideas in the second century. In the first, they were Jewish, Oriental, or Greek ideas. Among the forces and movements which formed the material out of which gnosticism grew four were especially dynamic.

(1) R. M. Grant believes that *apocalyptic Judaism* was the main source of gnosticism.[7] Dualism and eschatology were essential elements in apocalyptic Judaism; both became fundamental in gnosticism. Apocalyptists believed that the entire universe—the earth, the underworld, the heavens, and their inhabitants—were involved in a conflict between the powers of good and evil.[8] This present age was evil and corrupt, under the power of Satan, and growing worse and worse. Hope for the righteous lay only in the future. God would soon intervene, overcome Satan, and inaugurate a new age of righteousness and peace.[9]

(2) *Greek philosophy* furnished many ideas that later became systematized in gnostic systems. The universe was considered to be composed of a number of spheres surrounding and rising above the earth. Each sphere is ruled by a minor deity associated with planets. Human destiny is determined by these powers. The world, perceptible to the senses, is not the world to which man belongs; he belongs to the ideal world set above the spheres where God dwells. Man's hope was not for a resurrection but for an escape from this world through death. Man's spirit, which Stoics called a spark of divine fire, was imprisoned in this world and sought release from it. This conflict between man and the world became basic in most gnostic systems of the second century.[10]

(3) *Oriental and mystery religions* abounded in the first-century Greek world. They provided another source of developed gnostic thought.[11] These religions were intensely missionary. The most popular were the religions of Isis and Attis and of Mithras and Serapis. Mithraism was

THE QUESTIONS

peculiarly the religion of the soldiers. The mystery religions, aside from being dualistic, offered a way of salvation and addressed their gods as Lord and Savior. The initiate was marked on his forehead and described as reborn.[12] Gnosticism, when it became a movement, drew heavily from these religions.

(4) The final source of developed Gnostic thought which was current in the world of the New Testament was various *heretical Jewish sects*. Chief among them, perhaps, was the sect which lived near the Dead Sea and whose practices and beliefs we know through the Qumran writings. This sect laid great stress on asceticism and incorporated many elements of foreign religions. Grant thinks that most of the elements of the Iranian religion—specifically, the emphasis on dualism—were already present in the literature produced and preserved at Qumran.[13] Nearly all the elements found in later gnosticism were already present in the life and literature of these "Essenes or near-Essenes." [14]

The ideas which led to gnosticism, when combined with Christianity, were already present in the New Testament times. They were "in the air," the common heritage of the Greek world. Converts entered the Christian faith with a whole set of ideas, attitudes, and habits derived from their culture. Often, these proved a problem in their adjustment to Christian life and thought. We call these ideas "gnosticizing"; they constituted "gnosticism in the making."

However, these ideas alone did not produce gnosticism. It took the combination of them with a distorted version of the Christian gospel. We know of no gnostic system which was not related to Christianity and which did not claim to be Christian. Only one scholar, to my knowledge, has proposed that one version of one gnostic text is uninfluenced by Christianity.[15]

3. The Gnostic Systems

In the second century various gnostic systems and teachers attempted an amalgamation of the Christian religion with gnosticizing ideas. Most Gnostics did not think of themselves as Gnostics but as followers of their founders; thus, the systems were called Simonian, Valentinian, Sethian, and so forth. The name Gnostics, that is, the knowing ones, came from the opponents of the movement. Irenaeus, in the title of his work, used "gnosis" to cover those sects which shared common emphases and characteristics.[16]

It would be impossible within the scope of this work to discuss each system. The interested student may find a discussion of each system in any standard work on gnosticism under the names of Simon Magus, Menander, Saturninus, Marcion, Valentinus, Basilides, or the *Apocryphon of John* (to mention the best known).

4. Main Tenets of Gnosticism

Gnosticism has come to serve as a name for a great variety of ideas and doctrines.[17] The name includes a "constellation of religious phenomena."[18] It is "chameleonlike" in that its meaning changes when we move from one system to another, always expanding to include one or more new and borderline ideas. However, there was something about all these systems which made it possible for ancient and modern writers to treat them as one, to call them gnostic.[19] In spite of great differences, there were some common elements which were basic to them all.[20]

These common factors may be reduced to two. First and most important was a way of salvation and life which was designed to solve the problems of everyday living. Second, there was a mythology which sought to explain God, the world, and human existence.[21] The fundamental meaning of gnosticism is not found in its mythology. Various systems used mythological motifs in different senses.[22] The fundamental thing about gnosticism as it confronted Christianity was that it offered a rival way of life and salvation. We begin with mythology. Only as we have some conception of its mythology may we understand the basis for the gnostic way of life.

(1) *The gnostic myth.* We may use this term; Bultmann does.[23] However, there were as many myths as there were systems. Only in the sense that we are speaking of a composite picture of the common elements in the various myths can we speak of a gnostic myth in the singular.

The myth of two gods was an element in most gnostic systems. The true God was completely transcendent and unknowable. He had no contact with the world either to create or rule it.[24] He is hidden from all creatures and cannot be known except through supernatural revelation and spiritual illumination.[25] In most systems, this God was identified as the Father of our Lord Jesus Christ.

The other god was an evil god, the creator and ruler of the universe in which we live. In many systems, this god was identified as the god of the Old Testament, the giver of the Law, the corrupter of the Prophets, and the origin of all distortion and evil in the world.[26] The origin of this evil god is variously explained in gnostic systems. Usually he is thought to be the product of a primordial fall of a divine being, an emanation or product of the true God. This god, sometimes called the Demiurge, together with his sub-rulers, often called the Archons, is totally evil, ignorant, and anti-divine, a depraved creature of light. He stands in opposition to the true God and seeks to keep the spirits of men imprisoned in the world and matter (see below).

The myth of the hostile world or universe is common to all gnostic systems in some form. The world was created by the Demiurge and his Archons. The purpose of creation was to keep the divine sparks of life which are found in men imprisoned.[27] The universe itself is composed of earth, its lowest part, surrounded by several concentric heavens, either three or seven. Above these heavens is the realm of the fixed stars. The true God dwells either in the highest of these heavens or above the stars.[28]

Borrowing from Greek philosophy, each of these heavens is said to be ruled over by an Archon (i.e., Gk. for ruler) who guards his sphere to prevent any "Light Sparks" from passing through it on the way to reunion with God.

The myth of human existence is more uniform in gnostic systems. This is the heart of gnosticism; the justification for its way of salvation and life is to be found primarily in its conception of human existence. Man (only some men in some systems) is composed of two essential parts —one earthly and mundane, the other spiritual and extramundane. The earthly is also composed of two parts—body and soul. The spiritual part of man is called spirit; this is his true self, a portion of divine substance or a spark of light, held prisoner in his earthly self.[29] The spirit alone can be saved and the whole of the gnostic system is centered on the deliverance of the spirit and its reunion with the true God from which it sprang.

The unredeemed *Pneuma* (Gk. for spirit) is imprisoned in the soul and flesh which was created by the Archons to keep it captive.[30] The *Pneuma* thus exists in the body and soul "unconscious of itself, benumbed, asleep, or intoxicated by the poison of the world." [31] In brief, it is ignorant of itself and can only be awakened by knowledge coming by way of divine revelation or illumination.[32] Other names given to Spirit are Reason, Light-Dew, and Light-Spark.[33]

(2) *The way of salvation and life. Salvation through knowledge is the basic tenet* of gnostic systems. "Gnostic" comes from the Greek word *(gnosis)* which means knowledge. A famous gnostic saying is: "What liberates is the knowledge of who we were, what we became; where we were, whereinto we have been thrown; whereto we speed, wherefrom we

are redeemed; what birth is, and what rebirth."[34]

This knowledge is primarily *self-knowledge*. The definitive knowledge in gnosticism is the knowledge of "one's world-foreignness," the heavenly origin of the true self, and the way of deliverance from this hostile world.[35] Though this knowledge is sometimes called "knowledge of God," it is basically knowledge of the soul's way out of the world.[36] Thus the gnostic approach to life may be called a "passionate subjectivity"; the Gnostic counts the world well lost "for the sake of self-discovery."[37]

The *goal of gnostic salvation* is escape from the hostile world. It is the release of the "inner man" from the bonds of the world.[38] *In this life* the Gnostic comes to know himself as a heavenly being imprisoned in the body and soul. His self-knowledge helps him see that he does not belong to the world, that he is a pilgrim on his way back to his heavenly home. He was once born into the world; he is now reborn into the spiritual world.[39] He seeks freedom from the astral spirits, the God of the Old Testament, the Mosaic law or any law, and from the tyranny of creation.[40] His knowledge is more than an instrument of salvation; *it is itself salvation* in the world.[41] *At death* the spirit-self is liberated from the soul and body and begins its journey through the heavens to its original home. Equipped with knowledge of the passwords which will permit him to evade the Archons, the guardians of darkness, he leaves behind in each sphere the foreign accretions contributed to his soul by it. Finally, stripped of all accretions he reaches God and becomes reunited with the divine substance.[42]

The source of saving knowledge is heaven. Most gnostic systems had a redeemer figure which they identified with a Christ whose humanity was only apparent and not real. Some did not have a redeemer figure. But in all systems, knowledge came from heaven, sometimes through visions and revelations of various sorts.

The gnostic way of life was determined by hostility toward the world, but it took two directions or a mixture of the two—antinomian libertinism or rigid asceticism.[43] The ascetic believed that he must avoid further contamination of his real self by the things of the world and so avoided any contact with the world. The antinomian believed that he had absolute freedom from the world, that transgressions prohibited by the law affected only the soul and body and did not reach the *Pneuma* (spirit). His freedom was more than mere permissiveness; it was a deliberate flaunting of the authority of the Archons. He believed that his violation of demiurgical norms thwarted the designs of the Archons and actually contributed to his salvation.[44]

II. Paul and the Gnosticizers

Gnosticism *as such* did not exist in the New Testament times. Some —Schmithals, Schrottroff, and most German scholars—insist that it did. Their insistence is based on a modified definition of gnosticism which identifies it by one or more of its elements rather than as a system of thought. Walter Schmithals, for example, believes that any religious movement which teaches man to think of himself as a piece of divine substance is a gnostic system, no matter what else can be said about it.[45] However, we find this same thought in Stoic philosophy which is certainly not gnostic. But if we restrict the word to mean a system of religious thought, gnosticism did not exist in New Testament times.

First, no known gnostic document can be dated before the second century.[46] Of course, this does not prove that none ever existed. If one is discovered, we will have to modify our statement. However, the sources of our knowledge, though of necessity always incomplete, give us confidence in the truth of our contention.

Second, there is no evidence of a gnostic system of religious teaching in pre-Christian times. Many systems of thought—Philo, the Qumran sect, apocalyptic Judaism, Greek philosophy—embodied certain ideas which were later combined with Christian teachings into gnosticism, but none of them was gnostic.[47]

Third, none of the New Testament writers was gnostic. Both Paul and John have been accused of being Gnostics.[48] Both used terminology which later became gnostic and have teachings which are parallel to some gnostic teachings, but neither was gnostic in reality. Our discussion of Paul's answer to the Gnosticizers will show how far he was from being a Gnostic. The problem with many scholars is that they think a parallel is a proof of influence or source. This, of course, is far from the truth.[49] If one was influenced by the other, it is much more likely that the Gnostics were influenced by Paul's teaching.

It is much better therefore to speak of a "proto-gnosticism," an incipient gnosticism, or of gnosticizing tendencies as being present in New Testament times. We have chosen to use "gnosticizing" to describe those ideas found refuted in the New Testament which later were incorporated into gnostic systems. We use "Gnosticizers" to speak of those who proclaimed or promoted such ideas.

1. Paul's Confrontation with Gnosticizers

Some of the problems in the churches to which Paul wrote were caused by gnosticizing ideas. This is especially evident in Colossians and Ephesians. It is less evident that the ideas at Corinth were gnostic in any sense of the word. The pastorals (1 and 2 Timothy and Titus) show that Gnosticizers may have been at work in the congregations to which Timothy and Titus ministered.

Colossians was written to a church threatened with contamination of its doctrine *and* its life by a Gnosticizer. Paul warns the Colossians against being taken captive by "philosophy and empty deceit, according to human tradition, according to the elemental spirits of the universe, and not according to Christ" (2:8). "Philosophy and empty deceit" are two expressions for the same thing. It should be understood to mean, "a philosophy which is empty deceit." This expression indicates that the heresy in Colossae was a rather well-defined system of thought against which Paul was set.

"According to human tradition" identifies the heresy as involving certain Jewish elements. These are identified by the warning: "Therefore let no one pass judgment on you in questions of food and drink or with regard to a festival or a new moon or a sabbath. These are only a shadow of what is to come; but the substance belongs to Christ" (2:16–17). The use of circumcision as a figure for conversion (2:11) may point in the same direction.

"According to the elemental spirits of the universe" may or may not point to the hierarchies of Archons which later were incorporated into gnosticism (cf. 2:20). This same expression is found only four times in the New Testament (in these two passages and in Gal. 4:3,9). In the Galatian passages it refers to a relapse into Jewish legalism. Burton argues that the Greek should be translated, "the elements of the universe" and that the expression means "the rudimentary religious teachings possessed by the race." [50] This certainly fits in Galatians and would fit the context in Colossians as well. In any case, the expression indicates an attempt to introduce pagan elements into Christian thought.[51]

What some of these elements were is clear from Colossians 2:8–23. The fatal thing wrong with the Colossian heresy was that it was not "according to Christ" (2:8) and that the promoter of the heresy did not hold "fast to the Head" (2:19). In the first instance Paul points out that the philosophy has an inadequate view of Christ and his work (2:9–15). In the second instance, he points out that it has an inadequate view of the Christian life (2:16–23).

The Colossian teacher subordinated Christ to the "rule and authority" (2:10) or "the principalities and powers" (2:15). (The same Greek words are used in each passage.) Paul is careful to insist on the superiority of Christ to these entities. Paul's insistence that "the whole fulness of deity" dwelt in Christ "bodily" and that the Colossians had come "to fulness of life in him" (2:9–10) suggests that these truths were denied by the false teacher.

The kind of Christian life advocated by Paul's opponent in Colossae was a combination of three elements—Jewish legalism (2:16), angel worship (2:18), and rigid asceticism (2:20–23). Paul saw these practices as at best useless and at worst heretical.

Ephesians likewise gives evidence of gnosticizing influences. Paul's insistence that "every spiritual blessing" comes "from God" and "in Christ" (1:3) and that in him God has purposed to "unite all things" (1:10) indicates ideas which would belittle the person and work of Christ. His insistence that sin is the human problem and that salvation is by divine grace through the work of Christ (2:1–10) points in the same direction. His use of "mystery" to mean the gospel which is available to all sounds like a deliberate refutation of the validity of "inner knowledge" claimed by Christian Gnosticizers. His insistence on the dignity of the church as the sphere in which we gain the "full stature of Christ" (4:1–16) seems to be a denial of the validity of an esoteric fellowship.

Paul does insist that our Christian warfare is against "the principalities, against the powers, against the world rulers of this present darkness, against the spiritual hosts of wickedness in the heavenly places" (6:12). This sounds like gnostic thought. However, these powers are the promoters of antinomian libertinism in Ephesians and not, as in developed gnosticism, the givers of the Mosaic law with its moral teachings. It sounds like Paul has turned an argument back on its maker here.

The case of *the Corinthian correspondence* is one of the most hotly debated questions in New Testament scholarship today. Who were the opponents of Paul in Corinth—Judaizers or Gnostics? Schmithals [52] argues strongly that they were Gnostics; Schrottroff [53] insists that 1 Corinthians 1:18 to 2:16 is based on a conflict between Paul and a dualistic Christology and sees 1 Corinthians 15 as reflecting a conflict of Paul with dualistic anthropology.[54] Other scholars insist with equal vigor that the opponents were legalists like those in Galatia.[55]

Our conclusion: the opponents were not Gnostics, but they could have been Gnosticizers. First, gnosticism, as a system, did not exist in New Testament times. How then could Paul's opponents have been Gnostics? Second, elements commonly identified as gnostic were common in the Greek world of that day. The contamination in Corinth can easily be explained as the dilution of Christian teachings by the surrounding culture. This would not be surprising; the Corinthians were recent converts from that culture.

2. The Battlefronts

The plural is demanded. The confrontation of Paul with Gnosticizers was carried on on several fronts. Basically, these could be reduced to two: theology and practice. It is better to think of them as five, each one interacting on the other so that the answer to one problem has significance for the others.

(1) Concerning the doctrine of God, the following questions arose:

    Was there but one God or must the spiritual forces of wickedness be regarded as divine?

    Was God withdrawn from the world or was he involved in it?

    How did God relate his present activity in the world to the believer in his life and service?

(2) Concerning the person and work of Christ, these questions were urgent:

    Was Christ the final and supreme revelation of the true God or must further knowledge of God be sought?

    Was Christ a heavenly being or was he a part of the astral spirits who ruled the universe?

    Was Christ superior or inferior to the astral spirits?

    Was the humanity of Christ real or only apparent?

    Was the cross of Christ final in effecting man's salvation?

(3) Concerning salvation, the following questions were debated:

    Does man need redemption because he is a man or because he is a sinner?

    Is man in his totality saved or only a part of him?

    Is man saved in this world or only in the world to come?

    Does man receive salvation through knowledge or faith?

(4) Concerning the Christian life, several issues were at stake:

    Does life in this world have spiritual significance?

    Must the Christian practice asceticism in order to avoid contamination from the world?

    Is the Christian free from all restraint?

    What is the regulative motive and standard for Christian living?

(5) Concerning the church and its place in God's redemptive work, some questions were inevitable:

    Is the church important?

THE QUESTIONS 147

Are all members of the church saved or only an elite few?
Does the teachings of the church need to be supplemented by a higher and secret knowledge?

These are the battlefronts. The questions are before us. How did Paul answer them? This will now be our concern.

NOTES

1. R. M. Grant, "Paul, the Apostle," IDB, 3, p. 688.
2. R. M. Wilson, *The Gnostic Problem* (London: A. R. Mowbray & Co., 1958), p. 78.
3. Samuel Laechli, *The Language of Faith* (Nashville: Abingdon Press, 1962), pp. 252-3.
4. Cf. R. M. Wilson, *Gnosticism in the New Testament* (Philadelphia: Fortress Press, 1968); Hans Jonas, *The Gnostic Religion* (Boston: Beacon Press, 1958); R. M. Grant, *Gnosticism and Early Christianity* (Columbia Univ. Press, 1966); other works will be mentioned in our footnotes.
5. Wilson, *Gnosticism in the New Testament*, p. 85. 6. *Ibid.*, pp. 28-29.
7. *Gnosticism and Early Christianity*, p. 39. 8. M. Rist, "Apocalypticism," IDB 1, p. 158.
9. *Ibid.* 10. Wilson, *Problem*, p. 69.
11. Grant, *Gnosticism and Early Christianity*, p. 13.
12. H. G. G. Herklots, *A Fresh Approach to the New Testament* (Nashville: Abingdon Press, 1950), pp. 44-45.
13. *Gnosticism and Early Christianity*, p. 15. 14. *Ibid.*, p. 39.
15. Cf. Schrottroff (*Der Glaubende und Die Fiendliche Welt*, pp. 107 ff.) on Codex II version of the *Aprocryphon of John* 30:13 ff.
16. Jonas, *op. cit.*, p. 32. 17. *Ibid.*, p. 32.
18. R. M. Grant, "Gnosticism" IDB 2, p. 404.
19. Grant, *Gnosticism and Early Christianity*, p. 16.
20. Wilson, *Gnosticism in the New Testament*, p. 4.
21. Jonas, *op. cit.*, pp. 42-43. 22. Schrottroff, *op. cit.*, pp. 32-33.
23. *Theology*, I, p. 166. 24. Jonas, *op. cit.*, p. 42.
25. *Ibid.*, pp. 42-43.
26. Wilson, *Gnosticism in the New Testament*, p. 4; Robert Haardt, *Gnosis* (Leiden: E. J. Brill, 1971), p. 5.
27. Haardt, *op. cit.*, p. 6. 28. Wilson, *Problem*, p. 202.
29. Jonas, *op. cit.*, p. 49. 30. Jonas, *op. cit.*, p. 44.
31. *Ibid.* 32. *Ibid.*
33. Haardt, *op. cit.*, p. 6.
34. Quoted by Clement of Alexandria in *Excerpta ex Theodoto*, 78:2 with reference to Valentinianism. Cf. Jonas, *op. cit.*, p. 45; Haardt, *op. cit.*, p. 4.
35. Bultmann, *Theology*, I, p. 14. 36. Jonas, *op. cit.*, p. 45.
37. Grant, *Gnosticism and Early Christianity*, p. 9.
38. Jonas, *op. cit.*, p. 44. 39. Grant, *Gnosticism and Early Christianity*, p. 8.
40. *Ibid.*, p. 12. 41. Jonas, *op. cit.*, p. 35.
42. *Ibid.*, p. 45. 43. Haardt, *op. cit.*, p. 8.
44. *Ibid.* 45. Schmithals, *op. cit.*, p. 30.
46. Wilson, *Gnosticism in the New Testament*, p. 6.
47. Grant, *op. cit.*, IDB, p. 404; Wilson, *Gnosticism in the New Testament*, p. 71; Alan Richardson, *An Introduction to the Theology of the New Testament* (London: SCM Press, Ltd., 1958), p. 41.
48. Wilson, *Problem*, p. 75.
49. E. Earle Ellis, *Paul's Use of the Old Testament*, p. 82.
50. *Galatians*, p. 518. 51. Wilson, *Problem*, p. 78.
52. *Op. cit.*, p. 30. 53. *Op. cit.*, pp. 90-114.
54. *Ibid.*, pp. 115-154.
55. C. K. Barrett, "Paul's Opponents in II Corinthians," *New Testament Studies*, 17 (3, '71), pp. 233-254.

10
PAUL'S ANSWER

When we turn to Paul's answer(s) to the Gnosticizers, we are on more certain ground. What he had to say about Christ, about salvation, about the Christian life, about the church, and about God is plain to be read by all men. What his opponents had to say about the same subjects is reasonably clear from what he said.

But is the answer(s) Paul's? We must digress for a moment to consider that question. Colossians and Ephesians are sometimes called 2 Paul or deutero-Pauline. There is some justification for this opinion. There are apparent differences between these two letters and the ones we have been using in our discussion of the conflict with the Judaizers (especially Romans and Galatians). The differences are primarily theological and stylistic. It is said, and rightly, that the subject matter is different in these two letters. It is also said, and with some truth, that the style is different. The Greek is more polished; several long sentences occur.

Not all scholars reject Paul's authorship, though many do. H. Chadwick thinks the case against Pauline authorship of Colossians depends "upon a dubious assumption that the type of *gnosis* there combated cannot have arisen so early." [1] Reginald Fuller sees "no decisive reason for the rejection of Pauline authorship of Ephesians." [2] I join with these scholars in saying that the case against Pauline authorship is not proved.

If Paul himself did not write them, they were written by his followers who carried on his tradition and built on the foundation of his authentic letters. The theology is the same on either assumption.

Laying aside the question of authorship as unimportant, we turn to ask what Paul had to say about the subjects which were of vital concern in his opposition to the Gnosticizers.

I. The Involvement of God in This World

Later gnosticism tended to separate God from this world. From the mention of the worship of angels (Col. 2:18), it is likely that according

PAUL'S ANSWER

to the heretic at Colossae "God was to be conceived as infinitely remote from mundane things." [3] To some degree Paul agreed. The true God is the "Father of our Lord Jesus Christ" (Eph. 1:17; Col. 1:3). He is the "invisible" God, remote and unknowable (Col. 1:15). He is the one God; beside him there is none other (Eph. 4:6). His majesty is evident from the fact that "every fatherhood on earth and in heaven" derives its name from him (Eph. 3:15). "Fatherhood" is a better translation than "family." The apostle is maintaining that the very idea of fatherhood exists in God; every form of fatherhood is derived from this basic reality.[4]

Contrary to his opponents, Paul believed that God was involved in this world. He had created it (Eph. 4:6) and used it as the arena of his activity in achieving salvation for men. This was referred back, by Paul, to God's eternal, pre-temporal, purpose which had now come to be realized in the work of Christ and the salvation of believers. More than in his other letters, but not contrary to them, Paul stressed God's eternal purpose. The gospel is but the historical outworking of the plan for the ages which God has conceived in his own eternal purpose (Eph. 1:9; 3:9,11; Col. 1:27). Paul calls this a "mystery," using one of the words which was common in the mystery religions of that day. But he changed the meaning of the word. To the mystery religions, "mystery" was secret knowledge which was imparted only to the initiates. To Paul, "mystery" was an open secret. It had been hidden in the past but was now revealed for all men to see and know. Not only the gospel, but the salvation of individuals was the working out of a pre-mundane purpose of God, a purpose "before the foundation of the world" (Eph. 1:4). He destined us to be "sons" (Eph. 1:5; cf. 1:12). The Colossians are "God's chosen ones" (Col. 3:12).

The supreme example of God's involvement in the world is the coming and work of Christ. God's election was "in him" (Eph. 1:4), that is, it had his work in mind from beginning. God set forth his purpose "in Christ" (Eph. 1:9). The mystery, the gospel, is either "Christ in you, the hope of glory" (Col. 1:27) or "Christ himself" (Eph. 2:20). In Christ, God canceled the bond which stood against men and nailed it to the cross (Col. 2:14). Through the cross, he disarmed the "principalities and powers" and led them in triumphal procession as a sign of his victory (Col. 2:15).

The salvation of the Christian is also the work of God. Every kind of spiritual blessing comes to men from God through Jesus Christ (Eph. 1:4). This was according to his grace which he lavished on us in the beloved (Eph. 1:6–8). Salvation in its entirety is due to the act of God's grace (Eph. 2:8–9). God made us alive (Eph. 2:1,5–6); he qualified us "to share in the inheritance of the saints in light" (Col. 1:12); he delivered us from the dominion of darkness and transferred us into the realm of the kingdom of his "beloved son" (Col. 1:13). Through the cross of Christ, he reconciled us to himself (Col. 1:20).

Not only salvation in its beginning, but also salvation in its continuation in the Christian life was God's work. He is the source of "grace and peace" (Eph. 1:2; Col. 1:2). He is the true source of wisdom and insight into the "mystery of his will" (Eph. 1:9), the source of all kinds of spiritual wisdom and understanding (Col. 1:9). If converts had this knowledge, they would not covet a supposed higher knowledge. Again and again in these two letters, Paul stresses the need for the active help and support of God in living the Christian life. The readers are urged to "be strong in the Lord and in the strength of his might" (Eph. 6:10; cf. Col. 1:10). They are reminded that only the "whole armor of God" will suffice for victory over Satan (Eph. 6:11). But this power is already at work in them "in immeasurable greatness" (Eph. 1:19) and is available through prayer to a degree that is past their understanding or asking (Eph. 3:18).

This active and available power of God for Christian living is the basis of Paul's exhortation to prayer (Eph. 3:16,18), his insistence that they not "grieve the Holy Spirit" (Eph. 4:30), and his command to be "filled with the Spirit" (Eph. 5:18). He also asked that his Christian friends pray for him; the success of his ministry depended on the power of God. They were to pray "that utterance may be given me in opening my mouth boldly to proclaim the mystery of the gospel . . . as I ought to speak" (Eph. 6:19–20), and "that God may open to us a door for the word . . . that I may make it clear, as I ought to speak" (Col. 4:3–4).

There is little that is new in Paul's doctrine of God in this section. All that has been said could be duplicated in his previous letters. The new thing is the stress upon the involvement of God in the world. There is little doubt that this arose in opposition to a philosophy that tended to separate God from the world.

II. The Enlargement of Paul's Christology

The most important issue in Paul's confrontation with his gnosticizing opponents was Christ himself. The Gnosticizers tended to make Christ a demigod, or to use their terms, a demiurge. His contact with the world was made possible only because he was remote from the true God; he was thought to be less than the astral spirits which ruled the heavenly spheres; his death on the cross was not final; and his humanity was subject to question. Against these beliefs, Paul marshaled all his weapons.

What he says is a mixture of the old and the new. It is a "development of his former teaching," seeing the doctrine in "fresh relations," and "defining what had hitherto been left undefined." [5]

1. The Supremacy of Christ

There is no doubt in Paul's mind that Christ was absolutely supreme. He was no demigod, no "emanation from the remote God," but the manifestation of God himself. His work on the cross was absolutely final; he was the Lord of all creation, including the astral spirits. All things theological and practical were to be judged by their relation to him. One great passage about Christ (Col. 1:15-20) is no doubt a Christian hymn which was sung in the churches.[6] He quotes the hymn, not as something new, but as common ground with his readers. The problem in Colossae was that they were not letting the full implications of their own theology rule their thoughts. There are several other passages which contain concentrated teachings about Christ (Col. 2:8-15; Eph. 1:3-4,21-23; 2:4-7,12-21).

(1) *Christ and God.* "He is the image of the invisible God" (Col. 1:15). This is the first statement of the absolute uniqueness of Christ. It means we have a knowledge of the "invisible God" as he really is in Christ. The Gnosticizers thought that Christ was merely the beginning of such knowledge. Full knowledge of God came only in the remote future when one had learned the passwords which would gain passage through the heavens into the presence of God himself. Not so, said Paul. Christ gathers up in himself, in his own person, the full and perfect "likeness of God." [7] Paul adds, "In whom [i.e., Christ] are hid all the treasures of wisdom and knowledge" (Col. 2:3). The emphasis is not on the hiddenness but upon the revelation of these things in Christ. All that there is of God is to be known only in and through him.

To the same point is the statement of Paul that "in him all the fullness of God was pleased to dwell" (Col. 1:19; cf. 2:9; Eph. 1:23).[8] Colossians 2:9 states that this indwelling of divine fullness was and is "bodily"; this contradicted the tendency of the Gnosticizers to make the humanity of Jesus unreal. More important, these passages on "the fullness" (Gk. *plerōma*) imply the full deity of Christ. Later gnosticism used this term as a technical term for the "sum total" of the spiritual beings which bridged the chasm from the "immateriality of God to the evil world of matter." [9] If we may assume that the philosophy at Colossae already had such a system and used "the fullness" in the same way, Paul is contradicting their basic supposition that Christ was only one among these beings, perhaps the least. No. "In Christ resides 'the *total*' "; [10] all that there is of God is to be found in him.

Heaven is where Christ is "seated at the right hand of God" (Col. 3:1). God had exalted him at the resurrection "far above all rule and authority and power and dominion, and above every name that is named, not only in this age but also in that which is to come; and he has put all things under his feet" (Eph. 1:20–22). The "right hand man" comes from the custom in the oriental court of the vicegerent of the supreme ruler being seated at the monarch's right-hand. He was the executive officer of the kingdom. Paul used this picture to point to the supremacy of Christ over "all things." No angelic beings share in the rule of Christ; they are a part of the "all things" which are subordinate to him. Not just at the end of time, but already "now the exalted Christ is the Lord over all." [11] Christ stands supreme and unique. "He is no emanation of deity, for in Him the fullness of the Godhead dwells." [12]

(2) *Christ and the universe.* He is the "first-born of all creation; for in him all things were created, in heaven and on earth, visible and invisible, whether thrones or dominions or principalities or authorities —all things were created through him and for him. He is before all things, and in him all things hold together" (Col. 1:15–17). In this passage, four things are stated about Christ and the universe.

First, he created it. Nothing is omitted in the catalog of things which came into existence through his agency. His relationship is that of Creator to creature, not only to the world, but also to all angelic powers.[13] He is not a part of the universe, but "is absolutely superior to the . . . whole creation on earth and in heaven." [14]

Second, Christ is the Lord of all creation. This belief is expressed in the statement that Christ was the "first-born of all creation" (Col. 1:15) and "before all things" (Col. 1:17). In Christian history, these statements have been taken, by some, to show that Christ is not eternal in his being. He preexisted, but did not eternally preexist. Orthodoxy has rejected this interpretation and rightly so. In Jewish culture, the firstborn was the ruler of the family. The words should be taken in this sense here. The thought is of the absolute superiority of Christ over all creation. "As first-born he stands over against creation as Lord." [15] Christ as the first-born is "the natural ruler, the acknowledged head of God's household." [16] Any doubt of the correctness of this interpretation is dissolved by the statement: He is "the head of all rule and authority" (Col. 2:10). Plainly Paul is anxious to stress "the immeasurable superiority of Christ over whatever rivals" might be suggested by the false teacher.[17]

Third, Christ is the goal of all creation; "all things were created . . . for him" (Col. 1:16). Creation is relative. It finds its *raison d'être* in Christ.[18] The world is unable to impart meaning to our lives; it is unable to find meaning in itself. Only as the world comes under the kingly rule of Christ will it achieve its own completion and find true meaning.[19]

Fourth, Christ rules nature; "in him all things hold together" (Col. 1:17). The universe owes its coherence, not to a set of natural laws, but to Christ.[20] Natural law, a term invented by science to explain the orderliness of the universe, is really a name for the normal rulership of the universe by its Lord. He is what "makes it a cosmos instead of a chaos." [21] Christ is the "unifying bond" which holds all things together.[22]

(3) *Christ and his church.* In his relation to the church, Christ is said to be its "head" (Col. 1:18), its "foundation" (1 Cor. 3:11), its "all" who as the center of unity destroys all human distinctions (Col. 3:11), and the inner energy of its life by which the church grows (Col. 2:19; Eph. 2:20–22; 4:16). Paul multiplies figures of speech to insist upon the absolute supremacy of Christ over each church in the world.

"That in everything he might be preeminent" (Col. 1:18) is a summary statement. It speaks of the purpose of God that Christ shall be the absolute and final reality in everything—in relation to God, the creation, and the church.

2. The Finality of the Work of Christ

The work of Christ was complete; it needs no supplementation from any source whatever. In a word, it was final. While Paul had emphasized this fact in his previous letters, he is more emphatic than ever as he confronts the Gnosticizers. He insists that the climax of God's redemptive purpose is found in the work of Christ. The Jewish regulations were but a shadow of what was to come "but the substance belongs to Christ" (Col. 2:17). The turn of the ages had come in Christ; the law with its regulations had been only shadows of what God had intended.[23] Perhaps, this expression is based on the idea which was common in Greek philosophy of the "copy" and the "original." The "original" was thought to be the reality, but it could be reached only through the "copy." The philosophers at Colossae may well have incorporated these ideas into their teaching. If so, it is possible that they thought of "angel worship" (Col. 2:18) and "regulations" as copies through which they reached God.

Paul turns their language back on them. He admits that the "regulations" are only shadows, but Christ is the full substance. The shadowy things have lost their right to exist. The reality is shared only by those who adhere to the head of the body.[24]

The truth that Christ is the climax of God's redemptive purpose is stated in Ephesians 1:3–14. The work of Christ is the fulfillment of God's purpose which dates from "before the foundation of the world" (v. 4), is determined solely by God's will (v. 5), and is a "plan for the fullness of time, to unite all things in him, things in heaven and things on earth" (v. 10). Thus the gospel message is a way of making known to men the "mystery of his will, according to his purpose which he set forth in Christ" (v. 9). This "mystery," as we have noted, is the open secret which has now been "revealed to his holy apostles and prophets by the Spirit" (Eph. 3:5). It consists of "how the Gentiles are fellow heirs, members of the same body, and partakers of the promise in Christ Jesus through the gospel" (Eph. 3:6). Paul's apostolic commission is therefore "to make all men see what is the plan of the mystery hidden for ages in God" (Eph. 3:9).

As in his other letters, Paul focuses on the cross as the place where God's purpose was finally realized. Through Christ, God has reconciled "to himself all things, whether on earth or in heaven, *making peace by the blood of the cross*" (Col. 1:20, italics mine). In Christ "we have *redemption through his blood,* the forgiveness of our trespasses, according to the riches of his grace which he lavished on us" (Eph. 1:7–8, italics mine). He broke down the dividing wall of hostility between Jew and Gentile in order that he might "reconcile us both to God in one body *through the cross*" (Eph. 2:16, italics mine).

III. The Fullness of Salvation Now

Paul met all speculations about knowledge of higher worlds with the assertion that "nothing can surpass or supplement the forgiveness of sins." [25] Over against the philosophy which looked upon salvation as something yet to be attained and still undecided, Paul insisted that the believer has already received the fullness of salvation. The fact that the fullness of the godhead dwells in Christ bodily means "you have come to fullness of life in him" (Col. 2:10). "You have come to fullness of life" is an attempt to render in English the meaning of the Greek expression "you have been fulfilled." The tense of the expression is the intensive perfect, viewing the action as completed in the past with enduring results. There is a play on words in the "fullness" that dwells in Christ and the "fullness" the believer has received.[26]

Paul's habit in these letters is to speak of salvation as something accomplished in the past. God "has qualified us" for heaven (Col. 1:12), "has delivered us from the dominion of darkness" (Col. 1:13). "You were circumcised" (Col. 2:11). God made you alive with him (Col. 2:12); "you were raised with Christ" (Col. 3:1). God has "blessed us in Christ" (Eph. 1:3) and "made us alive" in Christ (Eph. 2:5). "By grace you have been saved" (Eph. 2:8). He piles up expressions to impress upon his readers the completeness of the salvation experience.

Not only is salvation complete in the sense of being completed in the past; it is also complete in the sense that it needs no supplementation in the future. More emphatically than ever, Paul emphasizes the fullness of the present salvation. It consists of every kind of "spiritual blessing" (Eph. 1:3). It means that we have been qualified (the Greek really means "been made worthy") of the inheritance of the saints in light (Col. 1:2). It means that we who were once dead in trespasses and sins have now been made alive in Christ (Eph. 2:5). It means that we have been rescued from the tyranny of sin and darkness and have been transferred into an entirely different realm of life—the kingdom of Christ (Col. 1:13). It means that we have been circumcised with a spiritual circumcision that consists of putting away the body of the flesh entirely (Col. 2:11; cf. Rom. 2:29). Could there be anything that surpasses a salvation that accomplishes all of that?

There is one peculiar expression found in Ephesians. The spiritual blessings which we have received are "in the heavenly places" (Eph. 1:3), and God has made us "sit with him in the heavenly places in Christ Jesus" (Eph. 2:6). This Greek adjective is found five times in this letter and nowhere else in the New Testament. In other passages, it means the place where Christ is seated at the right hand of God (Eph. 1:20), the principalities and powers "in the heavenly places" (Eph. 3:10) who are learning from God's grace to believers "the manifold wisdom of God," and "the spiritual hosts of wickedness in the heavenly places" (Eph. 6:12). The best translation is "the heavenly sphere." It is the sphere of spiritual activities, the immaterial region, the unseen universe which lies beyond the world of sense.[27] The striking thing is that Paul speaks of our present salvation as being in this sphere. His opponents thought of it as the sphere through which we must pass in order to reach God. Not so, said Paul. It is the sphere of our present fellowship with God in Christ. There could have been no better way to emphasize that salvation makes us here and now sharers of his dominion and dignity. Our life and thoughts are raised to a new and heavenly plane in him.[28] No one so vividly urges the reality of the Christian's union with Christ as an accomplished fact.[29]

Not much is said in these letters about the future hope of salvation. Present salvation gives assurance, for in it we receive the Holy Spirit which is both the seal of the completed contract and the foretaste of the future consummation (Eph. 1:13–14). Our life is hid with God in Christ and is therefore perfectly secure (Col. 3:3). "Christ in you" is the "hope of glory" (Col. 1:27). When Christ "who is our life appears, then you also will appear with him in glory" (Col. 3:4). This does not mean that Paul's eschatology had changed; it only means that circumstances called for stress at another point. When he does speak of the future, he speaks of it without any indication that he is introducing a strange and unknown concept.

IV. The Christian Life

How may one live like a Christian? This question was of great importance in Paul's confrontation with the Gnosticizers. Their influences are discernible in two directions—asceticism and antinomianism. Strangely, each of these grew out of the same soil—a dualistic concept of man. According to the opponents of Paul, man in his essential being was purely spiritual. This spiritual element was clothed in a material body which, in itself and in its activities, had no spiritual significance. This being true, one could say that human behavior had no spiritual meaning; it could contribute nothing to man's essential self and his relationship to God. Therefore, all regulations and standards are discredited. The outcome of that reasoning is antinomianism. Or, one could say, the body is a handicap to spiritual development. It constitutes a prison and its actions constitute a contamination of the spirit. To avoid further contamination, one must withdraw from the world, deny his normal appetites, and live ascetically.

Both conclusions were wrong because the assumption was wrong. Man is a total person; his whole being is related to God. Every action has spiritual significance. Paul therefore attacked asceticism with great vigor, and he attacked antinomianism with equal vigor. Neither was the answer to man's quest for the righteous life. The answer lay in bringing every action and relationship into harmony with our relation to Christ. He says: "As therefore you received Christ as your Lord, keep on walking in union with him, having been rooted in him and being continually built up in him and continuing to be confirmed in the faith just as you were taught, abounding in thanksgiving" (Col. 2:6–7, my paraphrase). The key comparison is: "as you received . . . keep on walking." The Christian life has the same nature as conversion. It is a life lived in submission to the lordship of Christ, and it involves the whole of man's life.

A life-style was to be judged by its conformity to the lordship of Christ in one's life. Submission to Jewish regulations was condemned because it failed to recognize that the turn of the ages had come; Jewish regulations were only a shadow of the reality which is Christ (Col. 2:16–17). Self-imposed religious practices [30] were to be rejected because they did not hold fast to the "Head" (Col. 2:18–19). Rigid asceticism was to be rejected because it denied the reality of our new life and demanded that we act as if we "belonged to the world" (Col. 2:20). Licentious behavior is to be shunned "for once you were darkness, but now you are light in the Lord; walk as children of light" (Eph. 5:8).

It is significant also that Paul has an extended section in each of these two letters on what might be termed domestic life. By this he was insisting that restriction of Christian living to moral and religious practices is invalid. Christian living encompasses the whole of life. It is concerned with the relation between husbands and wives, between fathers and children, and between slaves and masters (Eph. 5:21 to 6:9; Col. 3:18 to 4:1).

The details of Paul's moral and religious exhortations are very much akin to those in his previous letters and need not be repeated here. He was anxious that his readers see the full implication of their theology in their lives, that they resist any temptation to take a side road to a supposed "higher life" which would turn out to be an illusion.

V. The Church

No doubt, the opponents of Paul among the Gnosticizers belittled the fellowship of the churches. They were composed of people who had only the beginning of wisdom and knowledge. The true fellowship was the fellowship of the "elite," those who were "in on" the secrets of the universe. Paul attacked this attitude with a series of statements about the significance and primacy of the church which surpasses what he had previously written but does not contradict it.

So exalted is Paul's concept of the church in Ephesians and Colossians that most scholars find it impossible to think that he was talking of the local congregations. Therefore, the word "church" is said to mean the universal church in these letters with only a few exceptions. We have already discussed the impossibility of this with relation to the Greek word *ekklēsia*.

This is not to say, I repeat, that Paul did not have a concept like that of the universal church concept in our day. When he speaks of the reconciled Gentiles as being "no longer strangers and sojourners, but . . . fellow citizens with the saints and members of the household of God" (Eph. 2:19), this concept is what he had in mind.

But in the following verses (21-22), he is speaking of the local congregations. A literal translation of the Greek is: "in whom [i.e., Christ] each individual structure is joined together and grows into a holy temple in the Lord; in whom you also [as one such structure] are being built together in the Spirit for a dwelling place of God." The translation and the interpretation hinge on the use of a single Greek adjective, *pan*, meaning "every" when used with a noun without the article and "the whole" when used with a noun with the article. Here, it is used with a noun without the article and must have the meaning, "every individual structure" (cf. ASV). This use in the Greek is so well maintained in the New Testament that "only an absolutely intolerable sense can justify us in departing from it."[31] The context presents no "absolutely intolerable sense" to our interpretation and therefore it must stand. If this is true, all uses of *ekklēsia* in Ephesians and Colossians must be referred to the local congregations.

"He is the head of the body, the church" (Col. 1:18) is a metaphor which Paul finds meaningful in relation to the situation. In one way or another, this figure is repeated a number of times. (cf. Eph. 1:22; 4:2,16; 5:22; Col. 1:24; 2:19). By this figure, Paul wishes to emphasize the lordship of Christ over his church. Because Christ is the head, all other voices must harmonize with his or be rejected. He also wished to emphasize the uniqueness of the church. There is only one body (Eph. 4:4). Here Paul was speaking of the "one body" as "one kind of body," just as we often speak of the "family" as a kind of thing without reference to a particular family. He wanted his readers to know that there was only one kind of fellowship which God blessed—the church. To depart from it or to belittle it was to be less than Christian.

Paul has much to say as well about the life of the church as a creative fellowship, each member seeking the good of every other member. The human distinctions that separate are overcome in the life of the church, and Christ has become the center of unity (Col. 3:11). Their life together is described as one of compassion, kindness, lowliness, meekness, forbearance, forgiveness, and love (Col. 3:12-14). Their services which consisted of singing "psalms and hymns and spiritual songs" were to be for the purpose of teaching and admonishing one another in all wisdom (Col. 3:16).

Each member was to minister for the building up of the church. The equipment of members for ministry was the task of spiritual leaders which God had given (Eph. 4:11-12). The goal of such ministry was that all members might "attain to the unity of the faith and the knowledge of the Son of God, to mature manhood, to the measure of the stature of the fullness of Christ" (Eph. 4:13). The growing energy of the church was the indwelling Christ who supplied each member with his proper contribution. If each part of the church was working properly, under the lordship of Christ, the church would attain "bodily growth" and upbuild "itself in love." (Eph. 4:15-16) The urgency of the task lay in the presence of heretical teachers who threatened ruin to Christian children, that is, immature Christians. If the Christian did not mature, he would be "tossed to and fro and carried about with every wind of doctrine, by the cunning of men, by their craftiness in deceitful wiles" (Eph. 4:14).

NOTES

1. "All Things to All Men," *New Testament Studies,* May, 1955, p. 271.
2. Wright and Fuller, *The Book of the Acts of God,* p. 321.
3. Edwin Lewis, "Paul and the Perverters of Christianity," *Interpretation,* Apr. 1948, p. 148.
4. J. Armitage Robinson, *St. Paul's Epistle to the Ephesians,* (London: James Clarke & Co. Ltd. 2nd. ed., n.d.), p. 84.
5. J. B. Lightfoot, *Epistles to the Colossians and Philemon* (Zondervan reprint of 1879 Macmillan edition), p. 122.
6. E. Lohse, "Christusherrschaft und Kirche im Kolosserbrief," *New Testament Studies,* 11, p. 203.
7. C. F. D. Moule, *The Epistles to the Colossians and to Philemon* (Cambridge University Press, 1957), p. 62.
8. Moule (*Ibid.*) argues convincingly that Ephesians 1:23 looks upon Christ rather than the church as the fullness of God.
9. *Ibid.,* p. 165.   10. *Ibid.,* p. 166.
11. E. Lohse, "Pauline Theology in the Letter to the Colossians," *New Testament Studies* 15, p. 215.
12. H. M. Carson, *Colossians and Philemon* (Grand Rapids: Wm. B. Eerdmans, 2nd. ed., 1966), p. 18.
13. *Ibid.*
14. Eduard Lohse, *Colossians and Philemon* (Philadelphia: Fortress Press, 1971), p. 48.
15. *Ibid.,* p. 49.   16. Lightfoot, *op. cit.,* p. 147.
17. Moule, *op. cit.,* p. 66.   18. *Ibid.*
19. Otto Piper, "The Saviour's Eternal Work," *Interpretation,* July, 1949, pp. 294-5.
20. Moule, *op. cit.,* p. 67.   21. Lightfoot, *op. cit.* p. 156.
22. Lohse, *Colossians,* p. 52.   23. Lightfoot, *op. cit.,* p. 194.
24. Lohse, *Colossians,* pp. 116-117.   25. Lohse, *Colossians,* p. 40.
26. Lightfoot, *op. cit.,* p. 182.   27. Robinson, *Ephesians,* p. 21.
28. S. D. F. Salmond, "Ephesians," *Expositor's Greek Testament* (Reprint Edition, Grand Rapids: Wm. B. Eerdmans, n.d.), Vol. III, p. 288.
29. Moule, *op. cit.,* p. 9.   30. *Ibid.*
31. Salmond, *op. cit.,* pp. 300-301.

INDEX OF THEOLOGICAL SUBJECTS

1. God, 15–19, 34–35, 146–48
2. Christ, 32–34, 36–38, 44–49, 91, 148–50
3. The Holy Spirit, 129–32
4. Salvation-History, 19, 34, 85–92
5. The Law, 71, 86–89
6. Israel, 71, 89–91
7. Man, 19–23
8. Sin, 73–82
9. Grace, 82–84
10. The Cross, 33–34, 46–47, 92–94, 151–52
11. Faith, 94–99
12. Salvation, 27–31, 35–36, 49–50, 70–71, 101–11, 152–54
13. The Christian Life, 31, 56–57, 61, 72, 117–32, 154–55
14. The Church, 36, 50–56, 124–29, 151, 155–57
15. Hope, 110–15
16. Second Coming of Christ, 57–59
17. The Resurrection of the Christian, 59–61
18. The Future of the Christian, 61
19. Final Judgment, 16–17
20. Paul's Use of Old Testament, 23–25